Roy Wilding

ROMAN AMPHITHEATRES IN ENGLAND AND WALES

Published by 4 Corners Publishing

Published by
4 Corners Publishing 2005
2A Old Wrexham Road
Chester CH4 7HS
01244 679471

ISBN: 0 9545394 2 7

CONTENTS

ACKNOWLEDGEMENTS

I am pleased to acknowledge the help, support, kindness and generosity of spirit of the following people and organisations, together with those too numerous to list;

Penny Icke - Library & Reader services Branch, *Cofnod Henebion Cenedlaethol Cymru* – National Monuments Record of Wales (NMRW), Comisiwn Brenhinol Henebion Cymru – Royal Commission on the Ancient Monuments of Wales.

Katy Whitaker – NMR Enquiry and Research Services – National Monuments Record (NMR) – English Heritage.

Nina Steel – Sites & Monuments Record Archaeologist Ymddiriedolaeth Archaeolegol Gwynedd – Gwynedd Archaeological Trust.

Judy Miles & Laura Fielder – Corinium Museum, Cirencester, Cotswold District Council.

The Tupper family – Bignor Roman Villa, West Sussex.

Teresa Calver – Colchester Museum.

Mike Penney – Storm Photography.

Professor M. G. Fulford & the Society for the Promotion of Roman Studies.

Carolyn Wingfield – Saffron Walden Museum.

Chichester District Museum & the Guildhall.

Reading Museum Service.

David Ashford – The Dorset County Museum & The Dorset Natural History and Archaeological Society.

Vivien Knight – The Guildhall Art Gallery, London.

J. Waugh – Richmond Tourist Information Centre (TIC).

Neil Campling – County Archaeologist – North Yorkshire County Council.

Somerset County Museum.

David Algar – Salisbury & South Wiltshire Museum.

Amgueddfa Sir Gaerfyrddin – Carmarthenshire County Museum.

Chester Public Library and Cheshire County Libraries.

Chester Archaeology.

Grosvenor Museum , Chester.

Jane Ladyman – Chester Tourist Information Centre.

Galleria Borghese, Rome.

Margaret Warhurst, Maureen Smith, Gary Brown & Nathan Pendlebury – Liverpool Museum.

Christine Kenyon – CADW & CADW Welsh Historic Monuments Raglan Castle.

Eileen McCarthy- 4 Corners Publishing.

Sarah Rantou - 4 Corners Publishing

Gill Dunn - Archaeologist.

Gordon Emery - Local Historian

INTRODUCTION

Amphitheatre: Oval or circular building or arena with seats rising in tiers round a central open space

The amphitheatre should be viewed as a stadium that could be used for a wide range of uses. These probably included religious festivals, executions of criminals along with sports, games and ceremonial events. Other entertainments would include cockfights, hare coursing, bear and bull baiting, dog fights, equestrian events and animal hunts. Structures located in many English and Welsh amphitheatres have been interpreted as 'beast-pens' where animals were kept before the performances.

Amphitheatres are popularly associated with gladiators and gladiatorial combat. There is a considerable body of evidence, including inscriptions, images and a few pieces of equipment for gladiatorial combat in Roman England and Wales, and it seems probable that these amphitheatres were used for such events.

The shows held in Romano-British amphitheatres would have been on a much smaller scale than the vastly expensive and lavish entertainments seen in Rome, but were no less entertaining or important for the local population.

Amphitheatres were probably one of the most prominent and upstanding features in Roman England and Wales. However, with time and neglect their earthen banks would soon decay and the masonry be robbed for other uses. Nevertheless, excavation of the remains of such structures may lead to knowledge not only of the Roman period, but also to pre-Roman occupation of such sites. In the case of certain excavated amphitheatres evidence has been found of post-Roman occupation, thus helping to shed some light on the so-called Dark Ages.

Sadly, only Chester and London amphitheatres have been excavated using modern scientific methods and there is a dire need for these methods to be used on other amphitheatre sites in England and Wales.

SIZE (LONG AXIS) & DISTRIBUTION OF KNOWN ARENAS IN ENGLAND & WALES *

1.	ALDBOROUGH	59
2.	BAGINTON – THE LUNT	33
3.	BOSHAM	?
4.	CAERLEON	56
5.	CAERMARTHEN	50
6.	CAERWENT	44
7.	CAISTER ST EDMUND	38
8.	CANTERBURY	?
9.	CATTERICK	60
10.	CHARTERHOUSE-ON MENDIP	32
11.	CHESTER	58
12.	CHICHESTER	57
13.	CIRENCESTER	49
14.	DORCHESTER – MAUMBURY RINGS	59
15.	FORDEN GAER	?
16.	FRILFORD	45
17.	LONDON	62
18.	RICHBOROUGH	60
19.	SILCHESTER	46
20.	TOMEN-Y-MUR	33
21.	WALTON	?
22.	WINTERSLOW	38
23.	WOODCUTS	21

* ROUNDED TO THE NEAREST WHOLE NUMBER IN METRES

HISTORICAL OUTLINE

Origins of the Spectacles

According to Bomgardner 1, the Etruscan civilisation adopted the custom of gladiatorial combat (*munus gladiatorum)* from the Samnites of southern Italy, and then passed it on to the Romans during the period of the Etruscan Kings (6th century BC). Historical references among the Romans appear in the beginning of the First Punic War (264-241 BC).

In 264 BC, at the public funeral of Decimus Brutus Pera in the *Forum Boarium* (Cattle Market), his two sons staged a spectacle in which three pairs of gladiators fought simultaneously. Human sacrifices at the funeral of an important man were not new. The novel element was the introduction of armed combat ending in the deaths of the warriors. The blood of the victims was believed to enliven and sustain the shades (ghost or spirit) of the departed, who without sustenance would wander unsubstantially through the underworld without strength or memory.

Grief was not uppermost at these ceremonies, but rather a communal pride in the family and its role in shaping the destiny of the nation (*Patria*). The introduction of armed combat to the death into funeral rites may be seen in this light. An armed duel to the death would mirror the courage (*virtus)*, skill *(ars)* and success (*fortuna)* of the deceased. Initially, *munera gladiatorum* would have been intended to enhance the prestige and glory of the dead man as part of his family's and nation's glorious tradition.

During the later Republic, intense competition between eminent Roman families for a limited number of top jobs led to the degeneration of these original funeral rites in flagrant bribes for political support. Entrepreneurs arose who were eager to supply the ever increasing demand for highly trained professionals to fight as gladiators and Campania became the unrivalled centre of a regional network of gladiatorial training schools and barracks. It was from one of these institutions in Capua, owned by Cnaius Lentulus Batiatus, that the slave revolt led by the slave gladiator Spartacus erupted in 73-71 BC.

In 49 BC, Julius Caesar established his own training school at Capua. It accommodated 5,000 gladiators (*secutores)*, recruited from slave populations of the ever-expanding Roman Empire. Vast sums of money, that the top gladiators commanded, were paid to their owners/ trainers (*lanistae)* by Roman citizens hopeful of recouping such enormous sums when they successfully stood for public election.

Thus the era saw the transition of these spectacles from a religious rite for the illustrious dead to a popular entertainment of exploitation: votes being given to the politician who could make good on the promise of even bigger and better spectacles. Caesar's massed spectacles of 46 BC blew away the competition for sheer size and incomparable showmanship. Mass entertainment and 'spin' had arrived!

The life and death of a gladiator

The catastrophic eruption of Vesuvius in AD 79 created a time capsule of daily life in Pompeii, including hard archaeological evidence from training barracks about gladiators in the Flavian era. A large number of graffiti advertising forthcoming spectacles in the amphitheatre (*edicta munerum)* also survive. Professional sign painters *(scriptores*) daubed announcements on the exterior white washed walls of private houses. Seventy three notices survive, and they usually announced the name of the donor (*editor muneris, munerarius)*, the numbers of pairs of gladiators and often the troupe from which they came and the reason for the spectacles. A small number of inscriptions give an even more detailed glimpse of life and death in the arena.

One particular inscription details the complete programme and roster of the gladiators who fought in two series of gladiatorial shows given by the *lanista* Marcus Mesonius in the month of May, probably between AD 54 and 62. Papyrus programmes, similar to those painted on walls as graffiti, would have been on sale before spectacles, perhaps in the piazza surrounding the amphitheatre.

His name and his troupe affiliation identify each gladiator in a papyrus programme. Also entered is the type of gladiatorial armament he would wear and the number of combats he had previously fought. At a later date, another hand has added the outcome of each warrior's encounter, whether victorious (*vicit),* vanquished but granted life (*missus*) or dead (*periit).*

One section of an inscription records twenty gladiators who fought in the second series of games. Of these, ten were victorious, eight were beaten but spared, while another two died. Only 10% of the gladiators who fought in this show met their death. (However, what is not recorded is the number of potential gladiators who never even reached the arena and who may have been killed in training).

It was proclaimed that two gladiators had over 50 contests under their belts. If you were particular ruthless, brave, skillful and lucky the arena could be a passport to fame, fortune and freedom for a slave. The risks were grave, but the rewards were high. For the risk-taker the arena must have seemed a golden opportunity. For some of the losers it was literally the graveyard of hope!

Generally, gladiators belonged to one of two classes: the heavies and the lights. The inscriptions recorded a vast variety of gladiatorial armaments. Samnites (later called *secutores), hoplomachi* and *murmillones* were all types of heavily armed gladiator. These types had more or less a complete set of body armour, a helmet, a shield and a sword. These differed only in details of equipment design.

The *murmillo* often had a distinctive fish emblem on the crest of his helmet and was often pitted against a net fighter (*retiarus)*: a net to catch a fish. Being heavily armed offered better protection. However, the added weight of armour reduced mobility and agility, and also restricted fighting to short range. His was the 'waiting' game.

The lightly armed gladiator had the advantage of greater speed, agility and endurance. He used hit and run tactics and waited for an opening with the use of longer-range weapons; nets and trident *(retiarius)* or the long curving sabre of the thracian or else the two swords carried by the dimachaerius. Chariot gladiators (*essedarius)* had mobility of the chariot and long-range javelins. The horseman gladiators (*eques)* had small round shields and full-visored helmets and carried a lance.

The intention was for a finely balanced interplay between the varied strengths and weaknesses of light against heavy providing the most exciting combats, with the added incentive for heavy spectator gambling. At Pompeii the inscriptions record combats between *dimachaerii* and

THE COLCHESTER VASE (2ND CENTURY) GLADIATORS IN COMBAT. THE "RETIARIUS" OR NET- THROWER TO THE RIGHT INDICATES THAT HE CONCEDES DEFEAT BY THE HEAVILY ARMED GLADIATOR ON THE LEFT

PHOTO BY MIKE PENNEY: REPRODUCED BY KIND PERMISSION OF COLCHESTER MUSEUMS

hoplomachi, thracians and *murmilliones, thracians* and *hoplomachi, hoplomachi* and *murmillones.* However, those classes involving horses tended to fight with others of the same kind, either chariot gladiators (*essedarii)* or horsemen (*equites)*.[2]

Origins of the *Venationes*

The first recorded instance of the hunting of wild animals (*venatio)* in the circus as part of votive games (*ludi votivi*) occurred in 186 BC. Following Marcus Fulvius Nobilior victories in Greece, he celebrated games that he had vowed in return for victory. As part of the fulfilment of his vow, he sponsored a staged hunt of lions and leopards. This is the first record of a venatio where animals were killed.

By 169 BC the first recorded venatio (sixty-three *africanae* (big cats), forty bears and forty elephants) as part of a regular scheduled *ludi circenses* given by the annually elected curule aediles took place. The *venationes* now appear integrated into the fabric of spectacles of the Roman religious calendar, unlike the irregular triumphal games of *ludi votivi,* which where ad hoc performances.

The first reference to non-Roman criminals being thrown to the beasts for execution (*damnation ad bestia)* at Rome took place in 146 BC. Following celebration of his triumphal games for his victory over Carthage, Scipio Aemilianus put to death foreign auxiliary deserters from his army by throwing them to wild beasts (*feris bestiis*).

The earliest recorded instance of a *venation* in which multiple hunting displays with lions took place simultaneously (probably a circus) is recorded for the period about 100 BC.[3]
No gladiatorial spectacle (*munus)* was now complete *(iustum atque legitimum*) without wild beast fights that always accompanied them. It seems that other than success in battle, success in the hunt was the other prized attribute of a successful man. Thus in a single day all the cardinal virtues (courage, strength, skill, discipline) most prized by Roman society were on show for the enjoyment of the spectators.

The *venationes* took place in the morning before the main event of the gladiatorial combats in the afternoon. At Pompeii evidence suggests that normally these events were considered a poor second to gladiatorial fights. On the most part only local animals, such as bears and bulls – usually varying in format occurred (this may also have been the case in some or all of the British amphitheatres).

Trained professional huntsmen (*venatores)* would take on the animals let loose in the arena and the use of hunting dogs is recorded. Sometimes beasts were forced to fight one another by being tied together.[4]

Origins of amphitheatres

The original form of the amphitheatre probably took shape in wood in the middle of the Roman Forum during the 2nd and 1st centuries BC. This was the traditional venue for the gladiatorial combats in Rome. There is evidence people watched from balconies (*maeniana*) constructed especially for this purpose above the boutiques (*tabernae*) that lined two long sides of the Forum itself. Rome was certainly the place where the earliest attested gladiatorial combats occurred.

The earliest examples of stone amphitheatres occurred in Campania. Stone amphitheatres are found where either a Roman colonial origin (eg Pompeii – the earliest recorded stone amphitheatre circa 70 BC), or especially close links with Rome (Latin or maritime colonies). Often, a Roman military origin is a reasonable assumption. (Again, this may also have been the case in some or all of the British amphitheatres).

All the early examples of this genre are severely functional and business-like in form and use, and all share several features in common: exterior facades had bare walls, functional and with decoration. Seating was supported for the most part by earth fill consolidated between retaining walls or else by simple vaulting or some combination of the two. (These are typical features of all British amphitheatres except, perhaps, Chester).

At this early stage, arenas lacked subterranean galleries and service areas: a simple layer of sand covered the arena. Sophisticated cells *(carceres)* for releasing beasts directly into the arena had not yet been developed or incorporated into these structures.

The awnings (*vela*) which would later cover spectators did not come into use in the amphitheatre much before the mid-1st century AD. The colonnaded galleries, which later crowned the summit of the seating, are not found in these earliest examples.[5]

Functions of amphitheatres

The Colosseum (Flavian amphitheatre) does not truly represent most amphitheatres, because relatively few cities could afford such enormous and lavish buildings. The inhabitants of the Empire's less prosperous cities, small towns or other settlements who wished to have an amphitheatre, built instead simple, utilitarian buildings with an earth bank structure. It is this type of amphitheatre that was generally constructed in Roman Britain. The simplicity of Britain's amphitheatres has, perhaps, given rise to the false notion that the province's inhabitants were not interested in amphitheatres and did not enjoy amphitheatre shows.

Although British amphitheatres may have been modest structures, does not mean that they did not emulate the functions and social values of their more illustrious contemporary the Colosseum. In Bomgardner's opinion, the amphitheatre (Colosseum) had a multitude of functions and social values attached to it. 'Being seen' was almost as important as 'seeing' the spectacles. The predominant amount of seating space devoted to the upper and middle classes of Roman society segregated rigidly by class status in this structure leads Bomgardner to a number of conclusions:

> The Colosseum was a conservative monument extolling the traditional male virtues of courage (*virtus*), discipline (*disciplina*) and skill at arms (*ars militaris*). Vespasian (AD 69-79), like Augustus before him, was attempting to re-educate the Roman citizens and to re-direct and re-channel the potentially destructive energies unleashed in the arena. Vespasian tried to re-instill the ruling classes of Rome with the traditional military virtues and traditions that had made Rome great. He was a soldier, a no-nonsense, hardheaded pragmatist sprung from hardworking peasant stock.
>
> The Emperor would have approved of the vivid lesson of supremely professional military skill, courage and discipline even to the death represented in gladiatorial contests of the amphitheatre. In addition, the long tradition of hunting as 'warfare without armour' and as being worthy of adoption by the ruling classes for lessons it could teach about courage, skill, endurance and co-operative manoeuvres would also not have been lost on such an Emperor.
>
> Even the gladiators and hunters of the arenas, often drawn from the underclass of society, could in the arena become legends in their own lifetime.[6]

In addition, prisoners of war, criminals and enemies of Rome would meet cruel and agonising death in the arena. This not only issued a terrible warning to would be offenders, but also pandered to the sadistic 'bloodlust' of the spectators.

(Endnotes)

1 Bomgardner, D.L., The Story of the Roman Amphitheatre (2002), 32-34.
2 ibid., 56-57.
3 Ibid., 34-35.
4 Ibid., 57.
5 ibid., 59-60.
6 ibid., 31.

Seating by class and status in the Colosseum

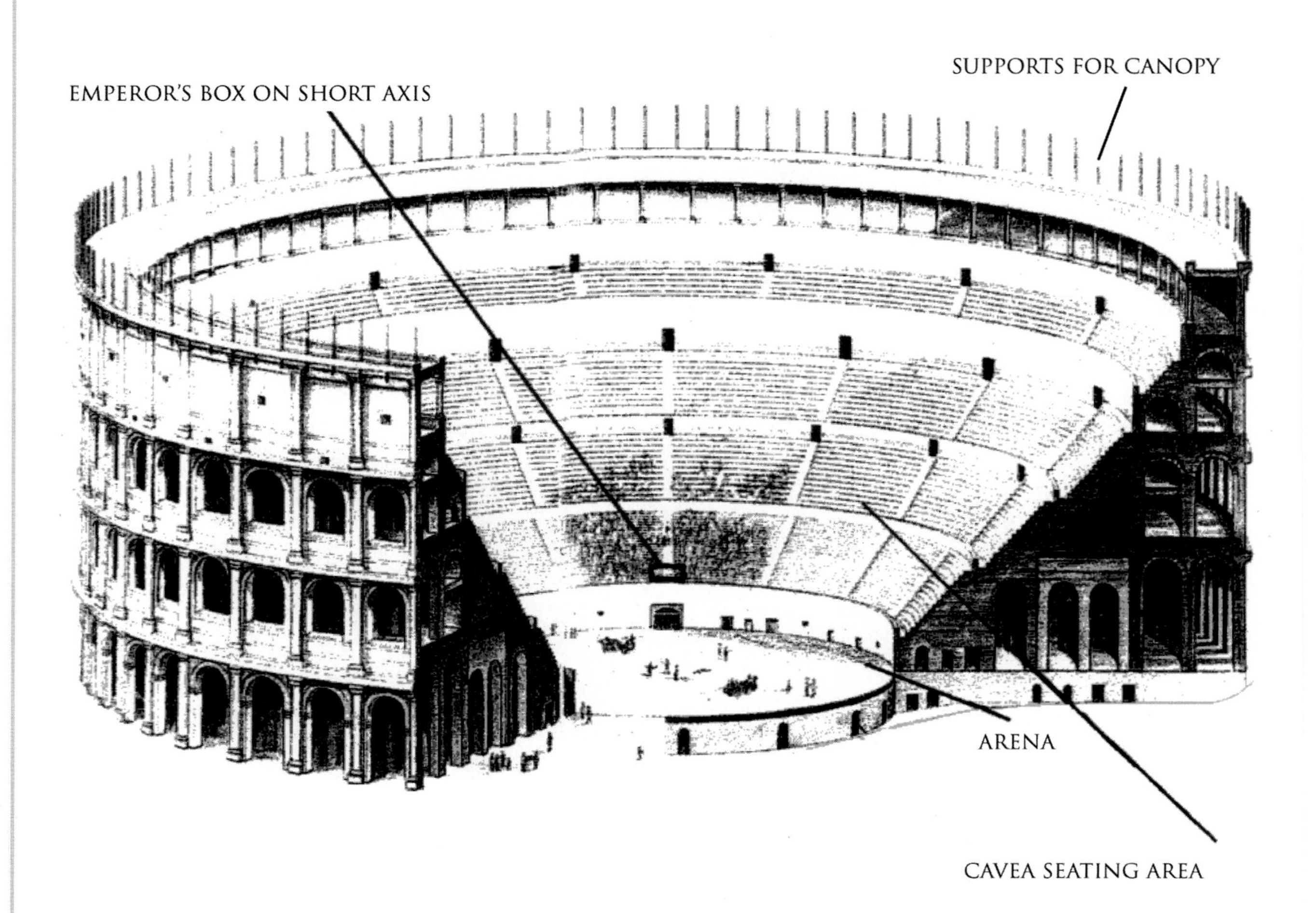

An elliptical arena was an immediate symbol of Roman inequality: high status people sat near to the arena on the short axis, thus providing a much better view than those high on the *cavea* and on the long axis. The seating arrangement was as follows:

Emperor's box: At the edge of the arena on the short axis - "To see and be seen".

Podium: At the edge pf the arena in the best seats - senators, priests of the most important religious cults (including the vestal Virgins), and distinguished foreign visitors and ambassadors.

Ima cavea: Higher up sat the knights.

Media cavea: Higher up still sat the Roman citizens.

Summa cavea: Even higher sat the undifferentiated mass of spectators crowded together.

Summa maenianum in ligneis: Finally at the pinnacle of the seating, protected by a tall colonnade, sat the ladies of quality.

ELEMENTS OF AN AMPHITHEATRE

Structural types of amphitheatres

The basic structure of amphitheatres varied and consequently these buildings have been classed into types according to the nature of their structure. The most recent classification scheme is that devised by Golvin, and the following description of amphitheatre structural types is a summary of more detailed discussions in Golvin's monograph.1 Golvin has identified two general structural classes, Type I and II. Type I is divided into two related structural subtypes designated Type Ia and Type Ib which include several variants.

Type Ia amphitheatres include those whose entire structure was carved out of a natural depression or incline, or whose arena was constructed by forming a large depression in the ground and whose cavea was supported on artificially created earth banks, much of the material for which was obtained from the excavation of the arena.

Buildings belonging to the related subtype, Type Ib were amphitheatres whose earth banks were subdivided into sections encased by walls. This was done in order to minimize slumping and shifting.

The front or inner slope of the banks of Type Ia and Type Ib amphitheatres was retained by a wall of either timber or stone which also served as the arena wall. However, the rear or exterior slope of the embankments was often not retained in any way. The seating of Type I amphitheatres could consist of stone or timber benches lodged directly in the surface of the banks, of timber bleachers supported on timber framing erected on the embankments or of stone benches supported on vaulting resting on the embankments.

The ease and economy with which Type I amphitheatres could be constructed made buildings of this structural type extremely popular. The Type Ia structure originated in the late Republican period and facilities of this type continued to be constructed until the end of the second century AD and perhaps as late as the third century AD. The Type lb structure appears to have originated at the end of the Republic and to have been perpetuated until the third century AD.

Type I amphitheatres were built throughout much of Europe but proved to be especially popular in Italy and the provinces of Gaul, Britannia (Roman Britain), Germania, Voricum, Pannonia, Moesia and North Africa. Because amphitheatres of this type were relatively easy to construct, the garrisons of military installations in frontier regions, inhabitants of small towns and the inhabitants of cities and settlements of modest wealth that wished to have an amphitheatre, built facilities of this type. However, this type of structure was suitable only for relatively small monuments as the embankments on which their seating rested were unstable when built up to any great height.

Amphitheatres belonging to the structural Type II are characterised by a cavea supported on a substructure of masonry walls disposed radially around the arena and roofed, in many instances, with vaults. It is in this manner that the truly monumental Imperial amphitheatres, including the Flavian amphitheatre or Colosseum in Rome and the amphitheatres at Arles and Nimes in France are constructed.

Amphitheatres of this type appear to have been constructed as early as the Augustan period (27 BC - AD 14). However, this structural type was not fully adopted until the Flavian period (AD 69-96). During which time the Colosseum, the monument that epitomises Type II structures, was built. From the Flavian period onward, Type II amphitheatres featured a wide annular corridor on the ground level immediately behind the exterior wall which communicated with various internal stairways and other circulation points enabling spectators to reach their seats.

Amphitheatres of structural Type II were constructed mostly in the wealthier cities of Italy, Gaul and North Africa with a small number of examples built in *Germania* and other Danubian provinces and Asia Minor. Construction of Type II amphitheatres ceased, as with Type I amphitheatres, in the third century AD as a result of economic decline.

Unlike Type I amphitheatres, Type II amphitheatres could be buildings of massive dimensions constructed on several levels. Moreover, they were monumental buildings while Type I amphitheatres were generally simple, unadorned utilitarian buildings with little decoration on the facade or outer wall. Type II buildings could be highly adorned; many possessed a facade or exterior wall consisting of two or more levels of arcades constructed of dressed masonry (*opus quadralum)* or brick.

The great number, at least 190, and visibility of amphitheatre ruins as well as their broad geographic distribution has led these buildings to be commonly considered the embodiment of Roman civilisation. Building Type I made its way into every region that fell under Roman domination from the late Republic onward.

Structural types of amphitheatres

Type Ia amphitheatres

TIMBER SEATING ON CONTINUOUS EARTH BANK

STONE SEATING ON CONTINUOUS EARTH BANK

Type Ib amphitheatres

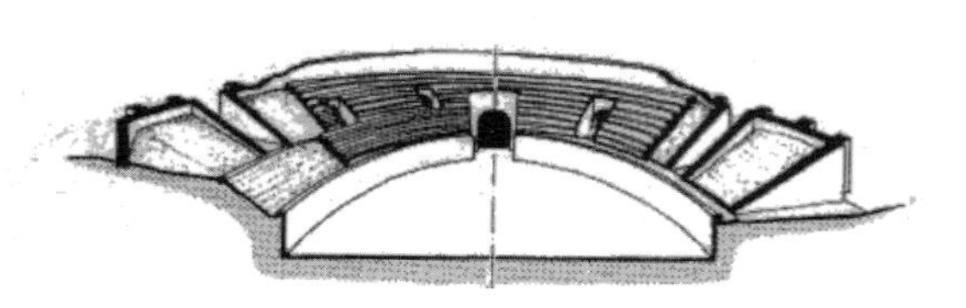

EARTH BANKS DIVIDED INTO LARGE SECTIONS BY RADIAL WALLS

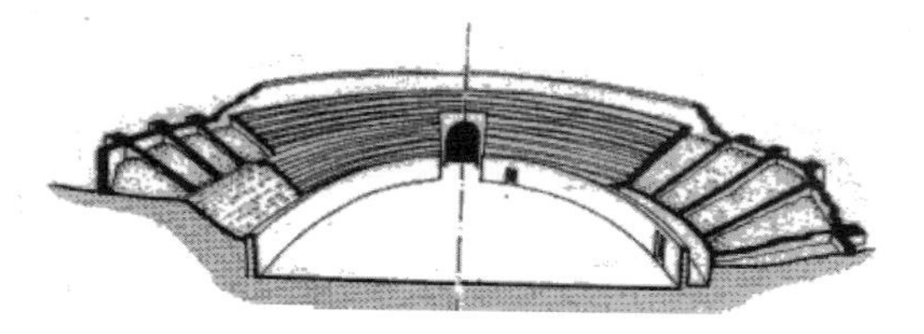

EARTH BANKS DIVIDED INTO SMALL SECTIONS BY RADIAL WALLS

Type II amphitheatres

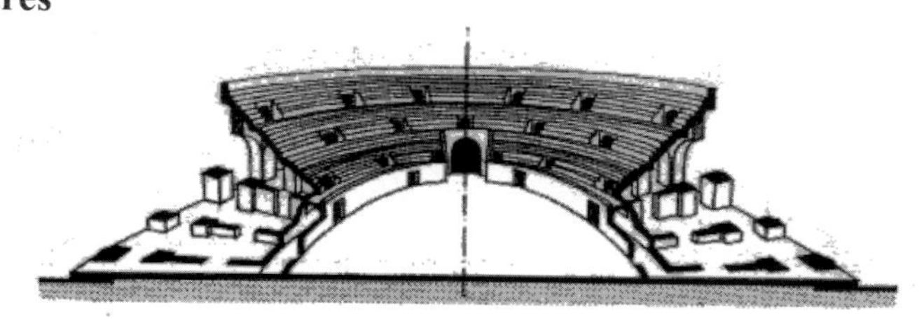

SEATING SUPPORTED ON RADIAL WALLS ROOFED WITH VAULTS

Location

As amphitheatres were such massive structures they were usually located on the outskirts of a fort, town or settlement. It was also a sensible arrangement to keep the large crowds that attended the shows from built-up areas, particularly within a fort, as a large assembly of people could soon turn into a mob and cause trouble or even insurrection. The site for the amphitheatre was chosen to provide quick and easy access and to limit the amount of excavation work required. Orientation of the amphitheatre appeared to depend on ground conditions alone, and varied according to the natural land features.

Arena

The arena was the principal element of the amphitheatre. It was an elliptical space in which the spectacles, gladiatorial games and venationes, took place. It was level and generally floored with sand (the Latin word from which the term "arena" is derived), a material which provided the gladiators with sure footing, absorbed the blood spilled during shows and was easily renewed. Its elliptical shape allowed combatants to move easily in all directions and permitted spectators to perceive the action to the greatest advantage. The spectators on the lowest tiers of seats were protected from bounding animals or other dangers by a high wall that enclosed the arena and usually topped by a balustrade (*balteus)*. The arena wall was frequently decorated in some manner as it served as the backdrop to the performances and was seen by all spectators.

The arena was not a true ellipse or oval, but was made up of segments of circles, of different radius and different centres, joined together smoothly to produce a 'polycentric *pseudo-ellipse'*.
Using segments of a circle had the practical advantage over a true ellipse, because using a true ellipse the inner wall would not be parallel to the outer wall of the façade and would involve continuous and laborous on-site adjustments.[2]

Pits, substructures and basins were found in some of the more elaborate amphitheatres of continental Europe and other regions of the Roman Empire. However, they are completely absent from the amphitheatres of Britain. Featured in the floors of some arenas were central rectangular or square pits holding animal cages and equipment for hoisting these cages to the level of the arena floor (*pegmata*) so that animals could be released. Included were complex and sometimes multi-level substructures designed to allow animals and props to appear anywhere in the arena. Occasionally, there were shallow basins connected to a water supply which are alleged to have enabled the staging of *naumachiae*, mock naval battles described in several instances in ancient literary sources.

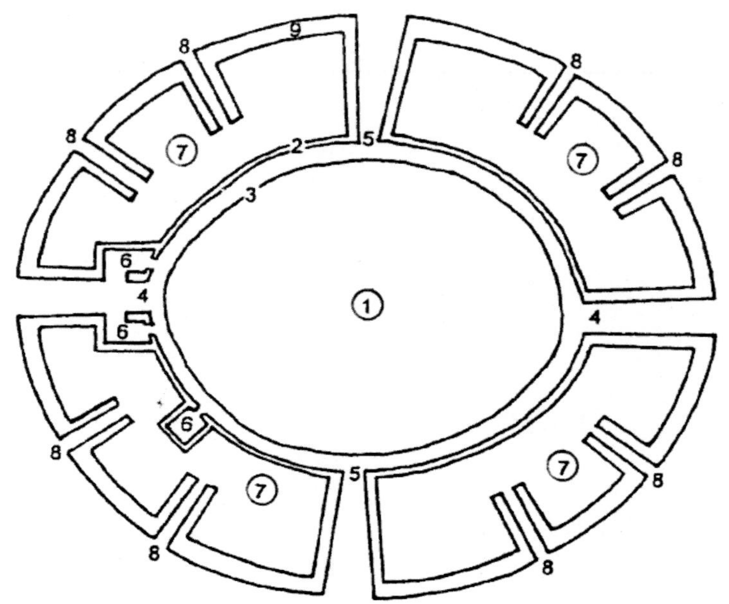

1. ARENA;
2 ARENA WALL;
3. EURIPUS;
4. PORTAE POMPAE;
5. PORTAE POSTICAE;
6. CHAMBERS SERVING AS BEAST PENS (CARCERES);
7 CAVEA;
8. VOMITORIA;
9. OUTER WALL

Drainage

Every amphitheatre tended to be liable to flooding because most arenas were sunk deeply below the prevailing ground level of the surrounding terrain, and there was a tendency for rising ground- water to accumulate in the arena itself. Also, whenever there was a shower of rain, because of the amphitheatre's funnel-shaped geometry, the run-off water also tended to pool in the arena.[3]

In general the drainage system consisted of two parts. The first part, the *euripus*, was a drain that ran around the entire perimeter of the arena at the foot of the arena wall and collected the rainwater that flowed down from the *cavea*. The water was, in many amphitheatres, channeled from the *euripus* to the exterior through main drains in the floor of the main entrances.

Safety Barrier

Some arenas, including the Colosseum's, (and perhaps, Maumbury Rings, Dorchester) were fitted with safety barriers. As arena-walls towered over 3m above the floor of the arena, the arena directly below its brow and around the periphery of the arena could not be seen by most of the spectators in the cavea, except those on the podium.

Animals or combatants in the 'blind-zone' would be invisible to most of the crowd and also a wild animal would tend to want to hide in this zone from the blazing sun and the murderous roar of a bloodthirsty crowd. The poor creatures would instinctively cower in terror and bewilderment in dark corners.

The solution was that massive posts were inserted into the floor of the arena and between them a strong net barrier was strung. This barrier not only helped the crowd view the spectacle safely, but also kept combatants and animals out of the blind-zone. It also added as extra protection for the crowd from wild animals that were good climbers. Behind the barrier was a broad gangway from where attendants could force the poor animals back towards the centre of the arena.[4]

Chambers

In those amphitheatres furnished with chambers serving as carceres, the carceres could occupy a variety of locations behind the arena wall. They were in many instances placed on either side of the arena gate of a *porta pompae (*main entrance). In this case they were designed to communicate both with the entrance passage and the arena, allowing for animals to be introduced in these pens through the doors off the entrance passages and to be released through the doorways communicating with the arena. Beast pens were, in other instances, placed at various points along the perimeter of the arena and designed to communicate solely with the arena. They were furnished with only one door which opened onto the arena and through which animals were both placed into the pens and released in the arena. In some of the more elaborate amphitheatres possessing a service corridor, the *carceres* located along the perimeter of the arena communicated both with the annular service corridor to their rear, from which some beasts could be loaded into the pens, and with the arena.

EARLY 5TH CENTURY IVORY FROM ROME DEPICITNG THE LEFT HAND LEAF OF A DIPTYCH. IT SHOWS A PRESIDENT WITH TWO COMPANIONS, PRESIDING OVER AN ELK HUNT IN AN AMPHITHEATRE (BY COURTESEY OF NATIONAL MUSEUMS LIVERPOOL, LIVERPOOL MUSEUM)

Entrances

The arena of an amphitheatre was accessible from the building's exterior. The main means of access to this area were the *porta pompae* located on the building's long axis and these consisted of wide ramped passages closed by a gate at the inner end. They were often roofed with vaulting that carried the cavea. These entrances, which were present in all amphitheatres were used both by performers and by attendants to bring equipment into the building. Moreover, it was through these entrances that the ceremonial procession (*pompa*) which paraded in the arena before the shows entered.

In some amphitheatres, there were also secondary entrances communicating with the arena (*porta posticae*). These could be located at either end of an amphitheatre's short axis or elsewhere along the perimeter of the arena wall and consisted of narrow doorways blocked by doors opening outward into the arena. In some cases, the *portae posticae* allowed people to make their way from the exterior of the amphitheatre to the arena. In other cases the portae posticae provided access to the arena from an annular service corridor located behind the arena wall or small chambers behind the arena wall which were generally either shrines (*sacella*) or animal holding pens (*carceres*).

Neither the service corridor nor the chambers communicating with the arena were universal components of amphitheatres but they were present in many of these monuments. The corridor, when present, was generally a narrow vaulted passage (about 1.5m wide) and was accessible from the passages of the *portae pompae* as well as through *portae posticae,* if these were present. These corridors served as waiting areas for performing gladiators and hunters from which they could emerge when their turn to perform came. Scenes depicted on 5th-6th century AD ivory diptyches suggest that, on the occasion of venationes, the service corridors were also used as places of refuge by hunters who would dart from the arena through the portae posticae, closing their wooden doors behind them to prevent pursuing animals from entering.

Cult shrines

Amphitheatres often possessed one or more small chambers that served as shrines and the location of these rooms varied. These recesses, which were commonly vaulted, were most often located behind the arena wall on a building's short axis, and communicated with the arena. In some instances, the shrine was not located on the short axis but instead on the long axis of the building, immediately against or at some distance from a side wall of a main entrance passage and was similarly accessible from the arena (e.g.at the *Nemeseum* at Chester). However, in a number of amphitheatres, a shrine might instead be found outside the monument, built against the exterior wall and flanking one of the *portae pompae* (*Nemeseum* at Caerleon). Whatever their locations, shrines were frequently decorated with niches for statues, wall paintings or marble veneer and many contained one or more altars.

These shrines could be dedicated to one, or two, of several deities associated with amphitheatres. These included Hercules, patron of strong and courageous men and Mars, god of war. Diana, patron goddess of the hunt (generally worshipped by the hunters or *bestiarii* who performed in amphitheatres rather than by gladiators). However, most were dedicated to Nemesis, the goddess of retribution, in which case the shrine was a *Nemeseum.* It is thought that the gladiators and the priests, who paraded in the *pompa* which preceded each spectacle, made offerings in an amphitheatre's shrine before the fighting began. Cupid gladiators are associated with the cult of the goddess Venus.

VENUS AND THE CUPID GLADIATORS

SECUTOR BEING ARMED (LEFT) RETIARIUS BEING LED TO THE FIGHT BY THE RUDARIUS (THE RUDARIUS OR UMPIRE CARRIES THE RUDUS - A WAND OF OFFICE) (RIGHT)

SECUTOR AND RETIARIUS FIGHTING ACROSS THE TOP OF A STONE CONTAINING A RING TO WHICH UNWILLING APPRENTICES WERE TIED, WATCHED BY THE RUDARIUS

SECUTOR ABOUT TO DELIVER A FINAL BLOW TO THE WOUNDED RETIARIUS

REPRODUCED BY KIND PERMISSION OF THE TUPPER FAMILY, BIGNOR ROMAN VILLA, WEST SUSSEX

Seating *(cavea)*

The arena, arena chambers and service corridor were all features connected with the performers and the performances that took place in the amphitheatre. The *cavea* or auditorium and its various components were features of an amphitheatre that were connected with the crowd who came to watch the spectacles. The auditorium consisted of tiers of seating ascending at an angle of inclination or rake sufficient to offer a clear view of the arena to the occupants of each seating row (generally about 25 degrees).

In many amphitheatres there lay at the very bottom of the *cavea* a wide platform (usually 3 to 4m wide) devoid of seating benches. This platform or podium was intended to accommodate the individual seats of local officials and eminent guests and was shielded by the arena wall's *balteus*. In some monuments, chief officials were able to sit in boxes (*tribunalia*) placed on the podium at either end of the arena's short axis. *Tribunalia*, always reserved for spectators such as the emperor in Rome or the *duumviri* in provincial towns, offered their occupants the best view possible in amphitheatres.

In the amphitheatres whose cavea included a *podium,* the *podium* was separated from the remainder of the *cavea* by a *praecinctio* or walkway. In the larger amphitheatres, the remainder of the *cavea* was subdivided horizontally and vertically. *Praecinctiones* or walkways subdivided the auditorium horizontally into zones or levels (*maeniana*) assigned to particular social classes.

Radial stairways (*scalaria)* descended at various points from the upper to lower portion of a *maenanum.* When the *cavea* was not subdivided into *maeniana*, the *scalaria* subdivided the upper to lower portion of the cavea seating into wedge-shaped blocks *(cunei)*. The more elaborate amphitheatres also had, in many instances, a covered gallery at the top of the *cavea*, in which women sat.

In the more elaborate amphitheatres, usually Type II, spectators could reach their seats by means of entrances consisting of internal staircases accessible from the building's exterior and which ascended, through the structure of the *cavea,* to openings at the different seating levels (*vomitoria).* Those monuments lacking *vomitoria* were usually provided instead with external staircases abutting the facade that permitted spectators to climb to the uppermost portion (rear) of the *cavea*; once in the auditorium, members of the audience descended *scalaria* to get to their seats.

1. PODIUM; 2 PRAECINCTIO; 3. FIRST MAENIANUM; 4. SECOND MAENIANUM; 5. THIRD MAENIANUM; 6. GALLERY; 7 SCALARIA; 8. CUNEUS; 9. VOMITORIA

(Endnotes)

1 Golvin, L'Amphitheatre romain, 75-76, 105, 109, 216-223, 270-274.
2 Bomgardner, D.L., The Story of the Roman Amphitheatre (2002), 25.
3 ibid., 80.
4 ibid., 20-21.

ALDBOROUGH

Aldborough (*Isurium Brigantum*)
North Yorkshire

Map ref: SE 406 664

How to get here

The village of Aldborough is off the B6265 near Boroughbridge. Part of the Roman site is beneath the village, partly under farmland.

Museum

A section of the wall and museum are managed by English Heritage.

What you can see

Earthbanks called Stud Forth Hill just a short distance from the southern corner of the city walls. **1**

Site History & Design Features

The amphitheatre has yet to be excavated. However, the remains were surveyed and drawn in 1930. The structure is thought to be a 2nd century, economically built Type **I** amphitheatre **2** that was roughly orientated east west. **3** The area of the monument closely matches that of Dorchester's amphitheatre in both shape and dimensions. **4**

Notes

1. Smith, G.E., A Guide to the Roman Amphitheatres (1984), 16
2. Golvin, L'Amphitheatre romain, 87, 91
3. Collingwood, The Archaeology of Roman Britain, 105
4. Golvin, L'Amphitheatre romain, 91

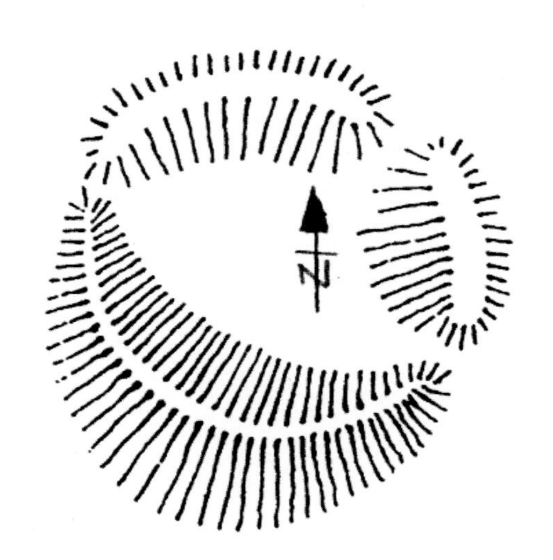

BAGINTON

Baginton – The Lunt

Map ref: SP 346 752

Warkwickshire

How to get here

The site is in the village of Baginton, just south of Coventry and near Coventry airport, accessible via the south-east end of the Coventry bypass.

Museum

There is a museum housed in the granary building.

What you can see

A stretch of the early ramparts, the east gateway and one of the granaries have been reconstructed, as well as the reconstructed *gyrus*.

Site History

The site was subject to systematic excavation and reconstruction, which began in 1966, by Coventry museum. The archaeology proved to be completely 'untypical' of a Roman fort. The eastern defences were found to curve to accommodate a circular *gyrus*, or training ground for cavalry mounts, 33m in diameter. It was clear that the fort was a cavalry base, constructed shortly after the Boudiccan revolt, perhaps as a base for the reprisal campaign. **1**

Notes

1. Johnson, D.E., Discovering Roman Britain (2002), 112

The Lunt

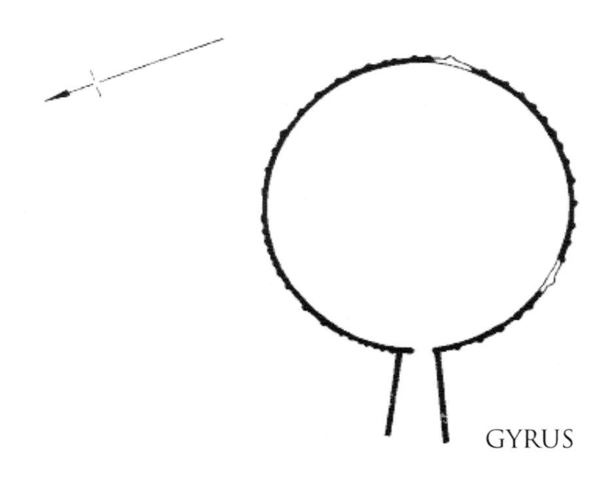

BOSHAM

Bosham (*Noviomagus Reginorum*)
Chichester
West Sussex

Map ref: SU 809 049

How to get here

The site is in the parish of Bosham on private farmland.

Museum and Tourist information

Chichester District Museum
Chichester
West Sussex
PO19 1PB
T: 01243 784683
F: 01243 776766
E; districtmuseum@chichester.gov.uk
www.chichester.gov.uk/museum

TIC T: 01243 775888

What you can see

Possible site of Roman amphitheatre, nothing is now visible. **1**

Site History

"About 150 yards (137m) southwest of this (a Roman villa: see also NMR Monument Wardens Report SU 80 NW 23) was a large excavation in the form of a basin.... Mr. Harris, whose family have resided in Bosham upwards of 200 years tells me that he recollect the spot before it was partially filled up and he has been told by members of his family that they remember remnants of the tiers of seats...". (Footnote) Mr. Lower thinks this much more likely to have been an amphitheatre. **2**

There are no traces of an artificial depression in the area of the above given siting, which falls within a pasture field. **3**

Notes

1. NMR Monument Wardens Report SU 80 SW 27
2. Rev. H. Mitchell, 'Sussex archaeological collections: relating to the history and antiquities of the counties of East and West Sussex': Sussex Archaeological Society 18 (1866), 2
3. NMR Field Investigators Comments F1 ASP 23- MAR-71

CAERLEON

Caerleon (*Isca*)
South Wales

Map ref: ST 3383 9034

How to get here

The site is 5km northeast of Newport and 2.4km from the M4 on the B4236. The amphitheatre is situated outside the western side of the Roman fort and is in the guardianship of CADW (Welsh Historic Monuments). **1**

Museum

Roman Legionary Museum
High Street
Caerleon
NP6 1AE

T: 01633 423 134
www.nmgw.ac.uk

What you can see

Caerleon is the best example of a complete Roman amphitheatre in both England and Wales.

Site History

The Roman legionary fortress of *Isca* was founded in about AD 74 or 75, during Julius Frontinus' campaigns against the *Silures*, a tribe situated in what is today South Wales. **2** It served from the time of its foundation until the late third century AD as the base of *Legio II Augusta*, the legion that moved from Gloucester in about AD 75. **3** Numismatic and ceramic evidence sealed within the building levels of the amphitheatre struture indicate that it was constructed soon after AD 77-78. **4**

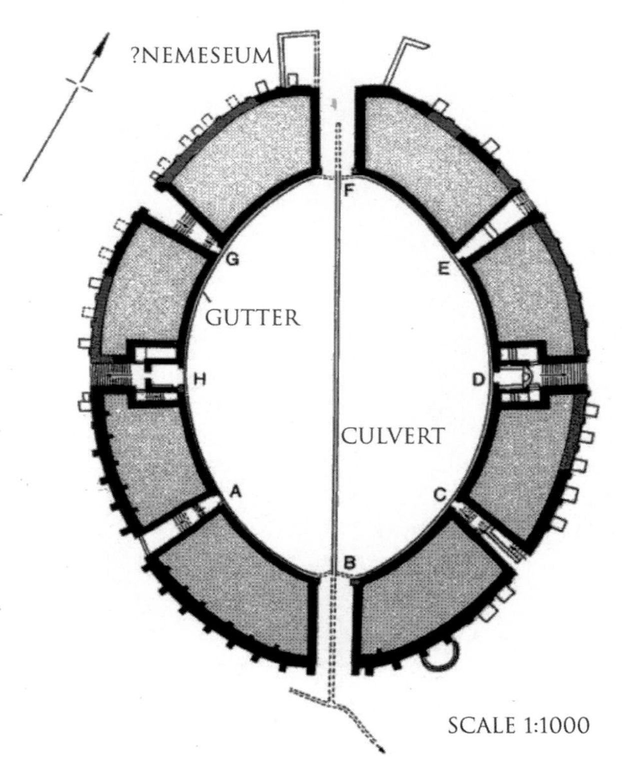

REPRODUCED BY KIND PERMISSION OF PROFESSOR M.G. FULFORD
AND THE SOCIETY FOR THE PROMORTION OF ROMAN STUDIES

The amphitheatre was built outside the fortress between the rampart's south-west gate and its south-west corner, in an open area flanked to the east by the fortress wall, to the west by a pre-existing bath building and to the north-west by a road leading from the south-west gate to the River Usk. The monument's size required that the rear of the bathhouse be remodelled and that the portion of the fortress' defensive ditch lying nearest the amphitheatre be partially filled to allow traffic to move round it. **5**

The amphitheatre was aligned with the fortress and oriented on a roughly north-south axis. **6** Its orientation resulted in the alignment of **Entrance F**, the *porta pompea* located at the northern end of the building's long axis, on the fort's southwest gate. **7**

Design & Construction

The method of construction of this amphitheatre was first to excavate the arena into the ground and then heap the recovered soil around it to form seating banks. Owing to the ground's southward slope, it was necessary for the builders to excavate the arena's northern portion more deeply. The southern half of the seating, because of the inclined terrain, rested on a bank built up almost entirely of material removed from the arena while the northern section of the seating rested on a less elevated embankment. An important feature of this amphitheatre was that a massive buttressed stone wall retained the exterior slope (rear) of the banks. **8**

Several entrances subdivided the embankments supporting the seating whose passage walls retained the earth banks; this characteristic signified that the structure was a 'Type Ib' amphitheatre, whose earth seating banks are subdivided into segments retained by radial walls. **9**

Arena

© Crown: CADW

The 'elliptical' sunken arena measures 56.08m by 41.6m on its long and short axis. The floor of the arena was initially covered with sand, but subsequently resurfaced with a variety of materials including packed earth and broken bricks. **10**

The arena was enclosed by a wall, which retained the front of the seating banks while supporting the bottom of their seating. This 1.2m thick arena wall was built of local stone in *opus incertum,* an inexpensive masonry technique. **11** The wall was built against the building's earth embankment, and is thought to have stood, including the stone *balteus* topped with a coping, to a total height of 3.7m. **12** The balustrades served to protect the spectators closest to the arena from escaping wild beasts. The coping blocks of the balustrade bear the sockets of a railing. **13**

The sandstone arena wall was covered with a smooth coat of hard mortar. **14** Typically, the arena wall was the most decorated and carefully treated feature of an amphitheater as it served as a backdrop or setting to the displays. The lack of a concentric wall behind the arena wall indicates the absence of a service corridor.

Drainage

The arena was provided with a drainage system consisting of a continuous peripheral gutter *(euripus)* together with a closed drain cut into the floor and crossing the centre of the arena from one *porta pompae* to the other. **15** The *euripus* was a straight-sided stone-lined channel, built directly against the foot of the arena wall and originally covered with a timber lid. **16**

The *euripus* was connected to an axial drain which was a stone-lined channel 0.75m wide by about 0.60m deep, probably originally roofed with wood. This ran a course from the northern *porta pompae* (**Entrance F**), passing beneath the ramp of the southern main entrance (**Entrance B**) to the exterior of the building, where it joined a drain running southeast towards the River Usk. **17**

RECONSTRUCTION OF AMPHITHEATRE
© Crown: CADW

External Wall

Just as a stone arena wall revetted the front of the amphitheatre's seating banks, so a thick stone wall also retained its rear. This exterior wall measured 1.4-1.8m and was similarly constructed in *opus incertum* using local sandstone. **18** This outer wall was plastered with a coat of hard cement in which false masonry joints were cored and filled with red paint to imitate brick dust mortar. **19**

It is has been estimated that the façade of the amphitheatre did not exceed 10m in height. However, it would have reached a sufficient height to provide an inclination of 25 degrees for seating and to have allowed it to be carried over the sloping barrel vaults covering the passages of *the portae pompae* and *portae posticae*. **20**

The outer walls were strengthened with buttresses and bolstered on three separate occasions. **21** The unbuttressed portions of the façade were decorated with pilasters to harmonise its appearance. In addition to adding strength to the structure of the monument, the buttresses may have served as a decorative feature; the scored and painted façade of the amphitheatre's façade and the arched doorways of the entrances would have also enlivened the appearance of the monument's exterior. **22**

Over time alterations were made to the exterior of the amphitheatre, including addition of a semi-circular flight of masonry steps built against the southern stretch of the outer wall, midway between **Entrance C** and **Entrance B** (south *porta pompae*) during the building's third modifications. It was constructed to provide access to the *cuneus* or seating block which could no longer be reached from the *vomitorium* to its north (**Entrance C**).

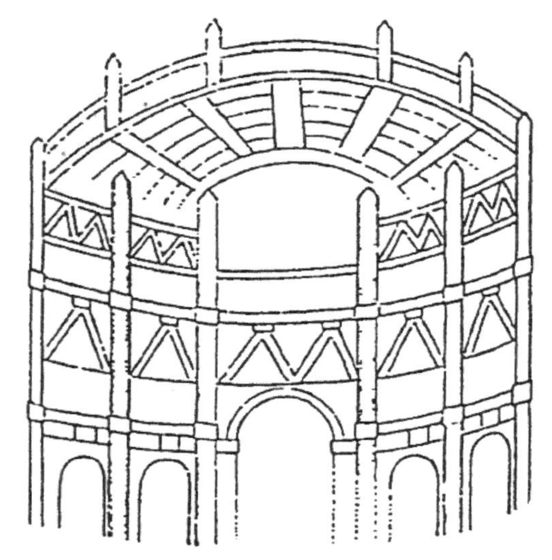

ILLUSTRATION FROM TRAJAN'S COLUMN OF A TIMBER AND STONE AMPHITHEATRE

CENTURAL STONE IN ARENA WALL © Crown: CADW

Seating

The seating banks, or *cavea*, were retained between the arena wall and the outer buttressed walls. The *cavea* varied in width from 12.3m to 13.6m due to the irregular layout of the outer wall. **23** The total dimensions of Caerleon's amphitheatre, including the *cavea*, were 81.4m by 62,7m. **24** There are thought to have been fifteen rows of seating (*gradus*), divided into eight *cunei* by the monument's eight symmetrically-placed entrances, and may have held 6,000 people. **25**

The excavated material to form the arena and to build up the seating banks was gravel, **26** but was not enough to elevate the proposed seating to the required height and angle; the banks stood at a height of 5.7m. Archaeological evidence suggests that the seating was supported on a timber superstructure anchored in the earth banks. Traces of timber were detected on the seating bank as an ash layer and, more recently, as two rows of post-holes. **27** The addition of massive buttresses to the exterior wall may have been in response to the strain caused on the structure by a timber seating framework, which may have 'capped' the stone outer wall (**see picture from Trajan's column**). **28**

Entrances

There were two *portae pompae* (**Entrances F & B**); two *portae posticae* or short axis entrances (**Entrances D & H**), and four *vomitoria* or seating entrances, one in each quadrant between the four principal entrances (**Entrance E & C** in the eastern quadrants, **G & A** in the western quadrants).

The *portae pompae,* or principal entrances, consisted of inclined ramps 4.8m wide, bounded by parallel side walls and roofed over their outer half with barrel vaults, several courses of which survive, whose angle of inclination (rake) corresponded to that of the passage floor. **29** These vaults were constructed of tufa alternating with bands of tiles and stone other than tufa. **30** The passage walls were constructed of local sandstone coated with plaster treated in the same way as that of the façade. **31** The ramps appear to have been partially resurfaced during later periods but the design of these entrances was never changed. **32**

Two *portae posticae,* or short axis entrances, provided both access to the arena and to the *tribunalia,* or boxes located directly over the entrances in which the senior officers would have been seated. These originally consisted of steeply inclined passages roofed with raking barrel vaults, which led from the amphitheatre's exterior to a small vaulted chamber (3m square) communicating with the arena beyond it.

Staircases on either side of each entrance's passage allowed spectators to ascend to the *tribunalia* and seating during the building's first phase. The northern staircase in each entrance passage, which was wider than its southern counterpart, would have provided access only to the boxes. The boxes' occupants would have entered the arena in the procession (*pompa*) preceeding the games. The southern staircase would have been used by lesser ranking spectators to reach their appropriate seating rows **33**

The short axis passages and chambers were initially constructed of a variety of materials. Sandstone and tufa were used for the walls and vaults respectively. Mortared courses of bricks were used to veneer the staircase faces of he chamber walls. Brick was also used to construct the archways above the chamber's rear entrances and above the lower opening of the staircases. Traces of plaster have been found on a staircase wall in **Entrance H**. **34**

Little is known of the appearance and design of the *Tribunalia* except that vaults roofing the chambers beneath them would originally have carried them and that they were probably demolished in subsequent modifications made to the entrances. It is possible that awnings may have shielded the occupants. **35**

The short axis entrances sustained extensive alterations, beginning with the raising of the ramps and the removal of the vaults in the Antonine period (Period II), undertaken in an attempt to stop rainwater from pooling at the bottom of the ramps. The problem

TOP: ENTRANCE A BELOW: ENTRANCE B © Crown: CADW

ENTRANCE H
© Crown: CADW

persisted, forcing the Romans to completely fill the entrance passages, with the exclusion of the chambers, with earth in the Severan period (Period III). **36**

The chambers remained in use during the amphitheatre's third period. The rear wall **of entrance D's** chamber, which was derelict at the time, was even rebuilt. The new wall featured a large half-domed niche, which may have been the location for the amphitheatre's second *Nemeseum*. **37** (See section on shrines below.)

The *vomitoria* were initially of uniform design, each consisting of a ramp or perhaps a flight of stone or wooden steps descending from an opening in the façade to the ascending stairs located toward the inner end of each passage. This staircase led to a very short landing at the level of the seating, from which a second steep flight descended to a 1m wide wooden door, attested by pivot holes in the sills of **entrances C and G**, communicating with the arena. **38**

The outer end of these secondary entrances was originally roofed with barrel vaults. They were like those at the axial entrances, an inner arch of which has survived *in situ* in **Entrance C**. **39**

However, the attempt to stop flooding failed, and the *vomitoria* ramps were finally raised to the external ground level in Severan times. **40** By being raised, they were converted into roadways leading directly to the gangway at the bottom of the seating. A new staircase, which would have allowed the crowd to climb directly to the *cuneus* at its north, was built in the outer half of **Entrance C's** passage. **41**

To gain access to the seating block south of **Entrance C,** the semicircular staircase previously described was built against the façade between **entrances B and C**. In addition, the inner end of **Entrance E's** passage, whose level was raised to that of outside ground level, was blocked by a retaining wall and then a small chamber communicating with the arena was built. It is likely that a timber gangway would have roofed the new recess and it may have served as a *carcer.* **42**

ENTRANCE F
© Crown: CADW

Shrines

During phase III of building, a roughly rectangular chamber was built against the outer wall immediately west of the **Entrance F**. This room contained a bench on the west wall and a platform in the north-eastern corner. Its position, furnishings and the discovery of a dedication to *Nemesis* inscribed on a thin leaden plate (about 7cm square) found in the debris of the northern half of the arena leads to the conclusion that this room may have been, in fact, a *Nemeseum*. **43**

The dedication is also known as the 'Caerleon Curse' and reads:

> 'Lady Nemesis, I give thee this cloak and boots. Let him who wore them, not redeem them, save by the life of his *sanguineus*'. **44**

The translator's reading *sanguineus*, 'bloody', relates to the colour of a horse, perhaps renderable as 'red chestnut': others are *aureus, igneus, roseus* etc. ('golden, fiery, rosy'). In Boon's opinion:

> The situation, then, was one age-old in magical practice, whereby Nemesis was given power over a competitor through the medium of his personal possessions. He was not to redeem them, i.e. safely get them back, unless his horse perished: and the understanding is that if his horse survived, he would not; or if he did, he would for ever be dogged by relentless fate. **45**

Finds

Direct evidence was found in 1909, in the form of facing-stone, relating to the possible use of the amphitheatre for gladiatorial games (*munera*). The stone shows the trident of a *retiarius*, or net fighter, upright between two curious shapes probably representing the flanged armour-plate worn by *retiarii* on the left shoulder; the design is closed by the palm-branches of victory on either side. **46**

Notes

1. CADW Monument Wardens Report MM232.
2. Nash-Williams, The Roman Frontier in Wales, 11-12
3. *Ibid.*, 11-12
4. Wheeler & Wheeler, 'The Roman Amphitheatre at Caerleon, Monmouthshire', Archaeologia 28 (1928): 146-147
5. *Ibid.,* 112-113
6. Fulford, Silchester Amphitheatre, 179
7. Golvin, L'Amphitheatre romain, 128
8. Boon, Isca, 92
9. Golvin, L'Amphitheatre romain, 140
10. Wheeler & Wheeler, Archaeologia, 115
11. *ibid.,* 118
12. M.V.Taylor & R.G.Collingwood, 'The Romans in Britain in 1926' JRS 16 (1926); Wheeler & Wheeler, Archaeologia 28, 115; Boon, Isca, 96
13. Wheeler & Wheeler, Archaeologia 28, 118-119
14. *ibid,*. 118
15. Grenier, Manuel. 3 II, 571
16. Thompson, Archaeologia 195 (1976), 151-152
17. Wheeler & Wheeler, Archaeologia 28 , 115
18. *ibid.*, 115; Thompson, Archaeologia 195, 157 181
19. Wheeler & Wheeler, Archaeologia 28, 118
20. Wheeler & Wheeler, Archaeologia 28, 116, 120; Thompson, Archaeologia 105, 231; Boon, Isca, 94
21. Wheeler & Wheeler, Archaeologia 28, 117, 130, 134, 139
22. Thompson, Archaeologia 105, 234; Wheeler & Wheeler, Archaeologia 28, 118
23. Boon, Isca, 93; Thompson, Achaeologia 105, 181
24. Boon, Isca, 93; Nash-Williams, The Roman Frontier in Wales, 173; Thompson, Archaeologia 105, 181
25. Graham Webster, The Roman Imperial Army (1979), 202
26. Taylor & Collingwood, JRS 16 (1926), 217; Thompson, Archaeologia 195, 161
27. Wheeler & Wheeler, Archaeologia 28, 117; Boon, Isca, 93-94

28. Boon, Isca, 96
29. Wheeler & Wheeler, Archaeologia 28, 121
30. Boon, Isca, 96
31. Wheeler & Wheeler, Archaeologia 28, 121-122
32. *Ibid.*, 121
33. *Ibid.,* 135; Boon, Isca, 97
34. *Ibid.,* 135, 139
35. Boon, Isca, 97
36. Wheeler & Wheeler, Archaeologia 28, 136, 138, 142, 153
37. *Ibid.,* 137-138; Boon, Isca, 100; Golvin, L'Amphitheatre romain, 81
38. Wheeler & Wheeler, Archaeologia 28, 122-123; Boon, Isca, 97-98
39. *Ibid.,* 128
40. Boon, Isca, 97-98
41. Wheeler & Wheeler, Archaeologia 28, 132
42. *Ibid.*, 134
43. ibid., 119
44. Boon, Isca, 100-101
45. *ibid.*, 100-101
46. *ibid.*, 99-100

CAERMARTHEN

Caermarthen (*Moridunum*)

Map ref: SN 4194 2064

South-West Wales

How to get here

The amphitheatre is located north of the A40, about 500m from the Tanerdy roundabout and is accessible to the public.

Museum and Tourist information

Carmarthenshire County Museum
On the A40, near Carmarthen,
T: 01267 228696

TIC T: 01267 231557

What you can see

Roman, possibly a theatre or amphitheatre, constructed against a hill, half hidden and partially reconstructed. **1** The western bank of the oval structure is laid out permanently and the arena wall reproduced in modern stonework. **2**

Site History & Design Features

When excavated, this 2nd century amphitheatre was found to be an economically built Type Ia earth-bank structure. **3** In addition, the builders of the monument were able to minimise labour costs by siting it on a hillside, cutting a semi-circular hollow to form its northern seating bank and using the removed fill to compose the now badly eroded southern bank. **4**

Excavation of the northern seating bank has revealed no rear retaining wall, which may imply that 2nd century amphitheatres were just as modest as their first century counterparts and lacked external walls.

The amphitheatre was located on the outskirts of the town and outside its defences. **5** It was built only 150m east of the presumed position of the town wall's gate. **6** The orientation of the amphitheatre lay on a roughly northeast-southwest line dictated by the contours of the hillside location. **7** The overall dimensions of the amphitheatre were 91m by 67m, with elliptical arena dimensions of 50m by 30m on its axes. **8** (It may be noted that the arena is particularly
'elongated' in plan).

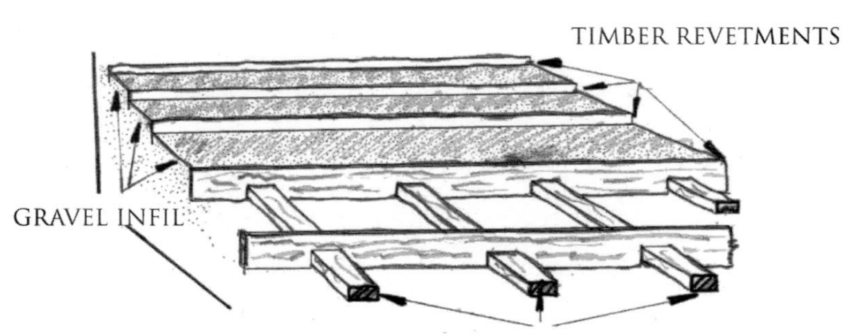

Drainage System

A particular interesting feature of this amphitheatre is evidence of a complex drainage system. The arena floor was found to have been covered with coarse-grained greenish sand and to have been ringed by a shallow 0.35m wide *euripus*; a 1.3m revetment wall constructed of stone on a clay pebble foundation enclosed it. The *euripus* constituted an element of a drainage system, which included a rubble-filled drain, intended to carry water from the hillside, descending the surface of the northern seating embankment and terminating beneath the arena floor. In addition, a rubble drain, identical to that on the hillside, was located directly beneath the arena wall and was found to traverse the arena opening of the east *porta pompae* providing additional drainage. Apart from their proper function the 'rubble drains' may have been designed as consolidating members on the northern *cavea* to minimise the risk of slip on the artificially steepened slope. **9**

Owing to lack of erosion on the northern *cavea*, actual traces of seating or terracing were found. This took the form of timber radial 'sleepers' or supports about 25cm square section, sunk into the natural shale at intervals of 1.3m running down the *cavea*. Across these were laid transverse timber revetments about 25cm high and 5cm wide; with the intervening spaces packed with gravel and levelled off to form terraced seating, each step was 70cm in width. Large quantities of iron nails found were probably used to secure these structural elements. **10**

Rough calculations of the amphitheatre's seating capacity, based on the area of the *cavea* and the details of the seating arrangements set out above, gave an estimate of between 4,500 to 5,000 spectators. **11**

Finds

A small fragment of Samian ware, probably Central Gaulish, dating from the first half of 2nd century AD was recovered from the seating bank. **12**

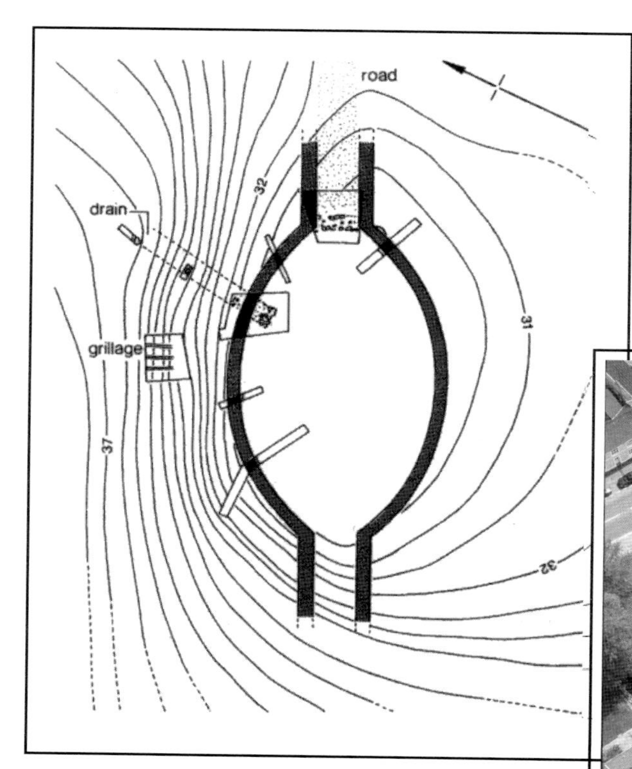

SCALE 1:1000

REPRODUCED BY KIND PERMISSION OF PROFESSOR M.G. FULFORD AND THE SOCIETY FOR THE PROMORTION OF ROMAN STUDIES

© Crown:CADW

© Crown:CADW

Notes

1. Cadw Monument Wardens report CM206
2. Johnson, D.E., Discovering Roman Britain, 137
3. Golvin, L'Amphitheatre romain, 87, 91; G.S.Maxwell and D.R.Wilson, 'Air Reconnaissance in Roman Britain 1977-84'. Britannia 18 (1987): 44.
4. Little, Carmarthenshire Antiquary 7 (1971), 58.
5. Wacher, Towns of Roman Britain, 51, 53..
6. G. D. B. Jones, 'Moridunum', PECS, 59.
7. Little, Camarthenshire Antiquary 7 (1971), 58, 61, fig. I.
8. Wacher, Towns of RB, 392 and Little, Carmarthernshire Antiquary 7 (1971), 58.
9. Little, Carmarthenshire Antiquary, 7, (1971), 58-59.
10. *ibid.*, 59-60.
11. *ibid.,* 60.
12. *ibid.,* 60.

CAERWENT

Caerwent (*Venta Silurum*)
South Wales

Map ref: ST 4699 9066

How to get here

8km west of Chepstow. The A48 from Newport bypasses the village, whose main street lies approximately on the east-west road of the Roman town. The site of the amphitheatre is located within the town walls in the northeast corner, about 30m from the north wall and 120m from the east wall.

What you can see

A possible Roman amphitheatre, a roughly oval stone wall enclosure, about 44m WNW-ESE by 35m, thought to represent an arena wall, with possible fragment of outer wall on SW; these features cut across earlier buildings and streets. **1**

Site History & Design Features

Caerwent is the last known amphitheatre to have been built in Roman Britain. **2** At an unknown date in the third century construction of the masonry was started. **3** It was a late addition to Caerwent, a town that had been in existence since the first century AD, which had emerged as the district capital during the Hadrianic period. **4**

Unusually, the amphitheatre was located in a built up area within the city defences, and constructed on the site of several buildings and of a road running north- south. **5** A level site was selected for the new amphitheatre, which measured about 59m by 52m and was roughly oriented east-west. **6**

Contrary to all known British amphitheatres, except Chester, the roughly elliptical space for Caerwent's arena was never excavated, nor does it appear that its *cavea* was constructed from earth banks. Also, the building's apparently unfinished state prevents a clear understanding of its structural attributes and type classification. **7**

The 0.6m thick wall surrounding the 43.5m by 36.3m roughly oval arena is the most substantial remains of the amphitheatre. Their complete absence on one segment of the northern circuit suggests that the building of the monument may never have been completed. **8**

The intention may have been for four arena entrances, of which the eastern main axis entrance and the southern short axis entrance were partially preserved. The east *porta pompae* is indicated by a 3.9m wide doorway with a door pivot *in situ* and the southern side of the surviving *porta pompae* extending towards the arena from the remains of the building's external wall. **9** Traces of the amphitheatre's external wall only consist of a short section on the south side at a distance of 7.5m from the arena wall, thus making it impossible to reconstruct the *cavea*.

Notes

1. Cadw Monument Wardens report MM001
2. Golvin, L'Amphitheatre romain, 274.
3. *Ibid.,* 139.
4. Wacher, Towns of Roman Britain, 375-376.
5. Ashby, A. E. and Martin, A. T., 'Excavations at Carwent, Monmouthshire, on the Site of the Romano-British City of Venta Silurum, in the years 1901-1903', Archaeologia 59 (1904): 105.
6. *Ibid.,* 108; Ward, Romano-British Buildings and Earthworks, 230.
7. Ward, Romano-British Earthworks, 230; Wacher, Towns of RB, 386.
8. Ashby, Hudd and Martin, Archaeologia 9 (1904), 104-105.
9. *Ibid.,* 105; Ward, Romano-British Buildings and Earthworks, 230.

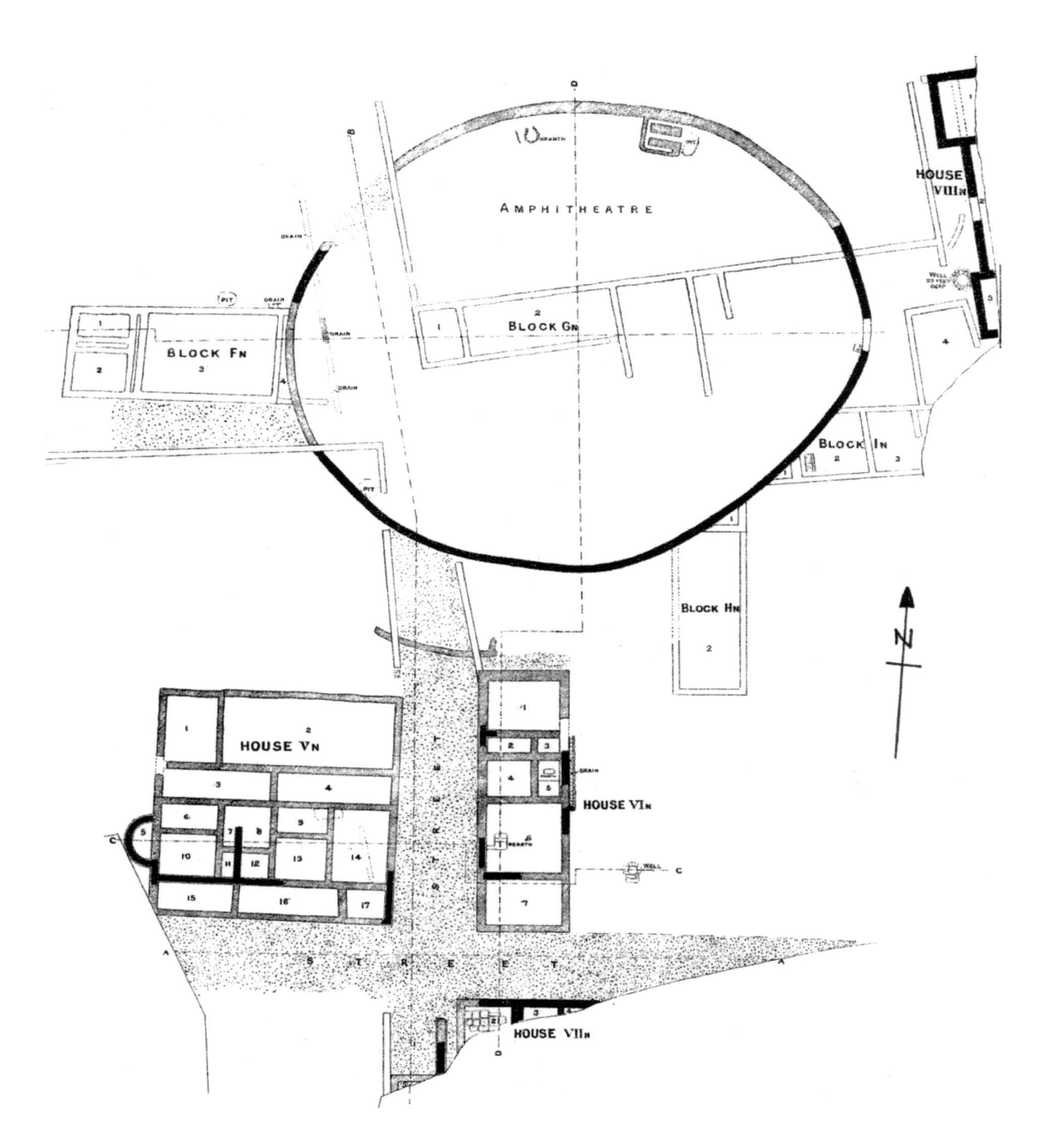

CAERWENT - PLAN OF HOUSES VN, VIN, VIIN & VIIIN, BLOCKS FN, GN, HN & IN, AND THE AMPHITHEATRE

CAISTOR ST EDMUNDS

Caistor St Edmund (*Venta Icenorum*)

Map ref: TO 2300 0310

South Norfolk

How to get here

The site is 5km due south of Norwich Castle, on a minor road from Caistor St Edmund to Stoke Holy Cross.

Museum and Tourist information

Norwich Castle Museum & Art Gallery
T: 01603 493636

TIC T: 01603 727927

What you can see

South of the Roman town of *Venta Icenorum* are two cropmarks situated on fairly flat arable land that indicate a possible amphitheatre and a Romano-Celtic temple. **1**

Site History & Design Features

Forced into subjection after their revolt under Queen Boudicca in AD 60-1, the Iceni were rehoused in *Venta Icenorum*, an administrative centre and market town constructed on the east bank of the River Tas about AD 70. Although today only the great ditch and impressive earthen rampart of the town are visible above ground **2,** in 1977 aerial reconnaissance photographs revealed the existence of a possible Roman amphitheatre and temple.

The amphitheatre cropmark is situated about 70m from the town's outer ditches and consists of a roughly circular bank approximately 14m wide and 60m in diameter overall. The north east quadrant of this bank is not visible as a cropmark and may have been eroded away. There appears to be a ditch within the bank about 10m wide, and there is a possible entrance on the west side of the bank. The temple cropmark is a regular feature approximately 9m square and it is suggested that it may be a Romano-Celtic temple, although there is no evidence for any internal features and nothing is visible on the air photographs. **3**

It appears likely that the amphitheatre may have been built during the 2nd century **4** and was a Type **I** structure. **5** The arena was slightly rounded and its dimensions were 38m by 32m, with an orientation of roughly north-south. **6**

Finds

Castle Museum, Norwich.

Notes

1. NMR Monument Wardens Report TG 20 SW 53
2. Johnson, D.E., Discovering Roman Britain (2002), 96-97
3. Aerial archaeology: the journal for air photography and archaeology 1 (1977), 17-18

CANTERBURY

Canterbury (*Durovernum Cantiacorum*) **Map ref: TR 1500 5741**
Kent

How to get here

Police Station on the junction of Rheims Road and the Old Dover Road

What you can see

Site now built over.

Site History

A late 1st to 2nd century Roman gravel pit overlaid by a gravel bank was exposed in 1964 when police headquarters was built. It was considered to represent "later adaptation as an amphitheatre". **1**

A trench dug along the north side of the police station revealed 1st/ early 2nd century pottery. The pit appears to have been used as a rubbish dump for a long time.
A mound of earth running from the north-east end of the station is believed to represent landscaping for a possible amphitheatre. **2**

Notes

1. NMR Monument Wardens Report TR 15 NE 166;
   Field Investigators Comments F1 FGA 27-JAN-65.
2. G. Andrews, Archaeology of Canterbury: An Assessment (1985), 57

CATTERICK

Catterick (*Cataratonium*)
North Yorkshire

Map ref: SE 2200 9900

How to get here

Head for Catterick racecourse, part of the amphitheatre is under the modern racetrack.

What can you see

The bank of the amphitheatre can be seen from the air as patchmarks on the racetrack.

Site History & Design Features

Roman Catterick was a small town that developed near a Roman fort. The fort, founded by Agricola in AD 80, was situated south of the River Swale on Dere Street; the road from York (*Eburacum)* to Corbridge (*Corstopitum*), Northumberland. It remained a military installation with some interruptions perhaps as late as the 4th century. **1**

The civilian settlement began to develop in the last 40 years of the 2nd century to the east and south-east of the fort and north of the River Swale. Ceramic evidence, including Samian ware, from the arena indicates that it is also during this period of initial growth, towards the end of the 2nd century that the amphitheatre was built. The hamlet was finally deserted in the 5th century before the main Anglo-Saxon migration to the area. **2** The monument lay about 900m south of the Roman agglomeration (beneath what is now the racecourse) and west of the Agricolan fort. **3**

In 1995, the north east section of the amphitheatre was discovered during archaeological investigations of the inside of the modern racetrack, and it was cleared together with a small adjoining area of the arena. However, the orientation of the structure has not yet been established because of insufficient excavation. The amphitheatre was built on level ground on a large natural deposit of gravel that provided the material for the embankments. **4** In addition, the arena floor appears to have been finely cobbled. **5**

Catterick may have been one of the largest of the province's amphitheaters, and it is estimated to have had an overall diameter of 140m. The seating banks were unusually wide, measuring 40m at their widest point. **6**

Notes

1. Wacher, *'Cataractonium'*, Princeton Encyclopedia of Classical sites, 208
2. Moloney, C., 'Catterick Race Course', Current Archaeology, 148 (1996), 130
3. *Ibid.,* 128
4. *Ibid.,* 128-129
5. *Ibid.,* 130
6. Vatcher, Antiquaries Journal 43 (1963), 199

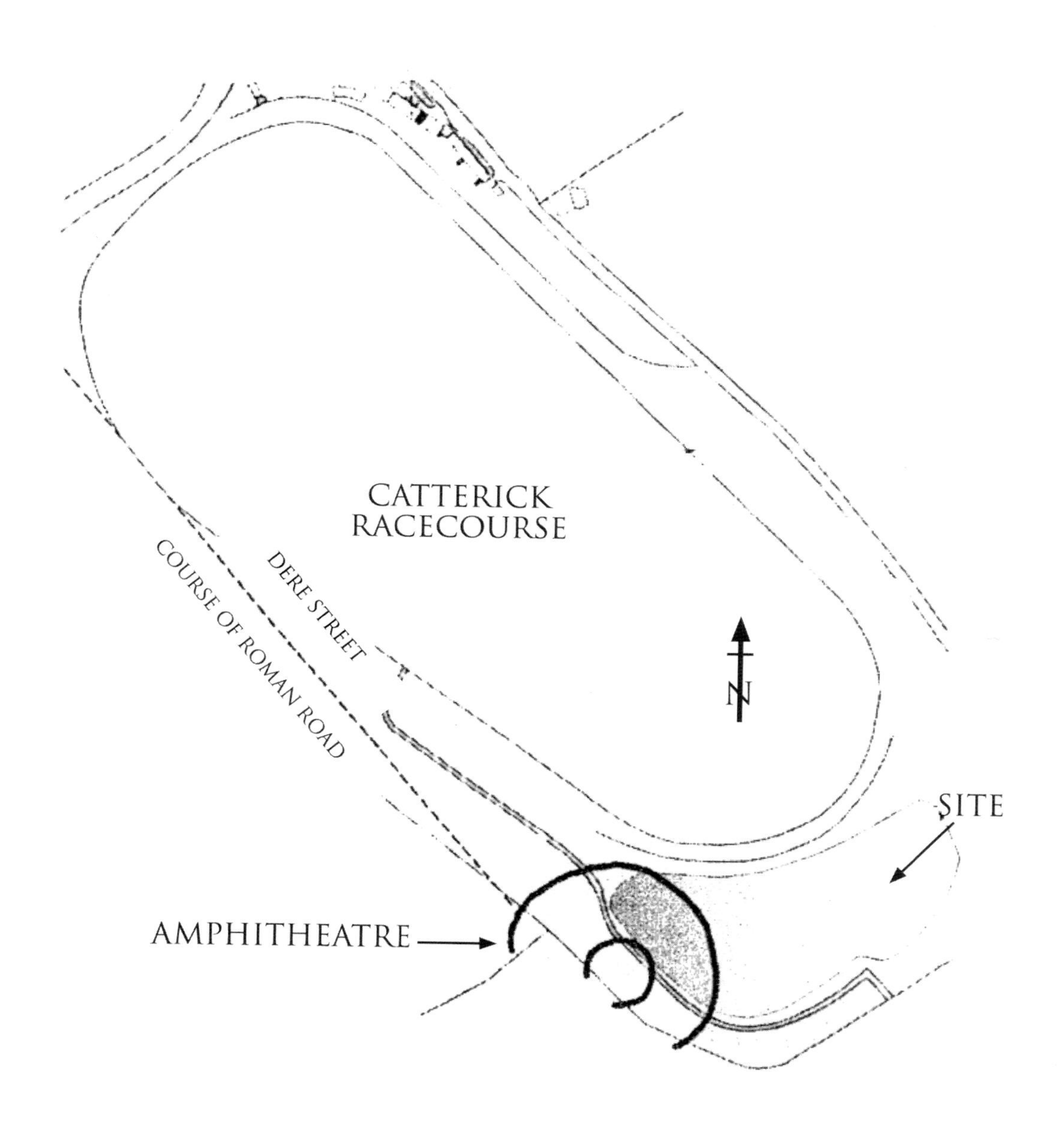
CATTERICK
RACECOURSE
DERE STREET
COURSE OF ROMAN ROAD
N
SITE
AMPHITHEATRE

CHARTER HOUSE- ON-MENDIP

Charterhouse-on-Mendip

Map ref: ST 4988 5651

Somerset

How to get here

The site is south of the B3134 between Burrington Combe and the Castle of Comfort Inn, northwest of its junction with the B3371.

Museum and Tourist information

Somerset County Museum
Taunton Castle
Castle Green
Taunton
TA1 4AA
Somerset

T: 01823 320 201
F: 01823 320 229
www.somerset.gov.uk/museums

TIC T: 01823 336344

What you can see

Earthwork enclosure comprising a large circular depression surrounded by a bank. Excavations in 1909 and 1938 did not yield conclusive results, but finds suggest a Roman date, and an amphitheatre is thought to be the most plausible interpretation. **1**

Site History

In a few years of the Roman conquest the silver and lead workings, which had been exploited during the Iron Age, were developed under Roman military supervision. Visible remains include at least one fort, an extensive area of mine workings and a small amphitheatre. **2**

During excavations in 1906, the earthwork was found to have two entrances, roughly on an east- west alignment. **3** Also found at all levels were flints and small Roman pottery sherds including Samian ware. **4**

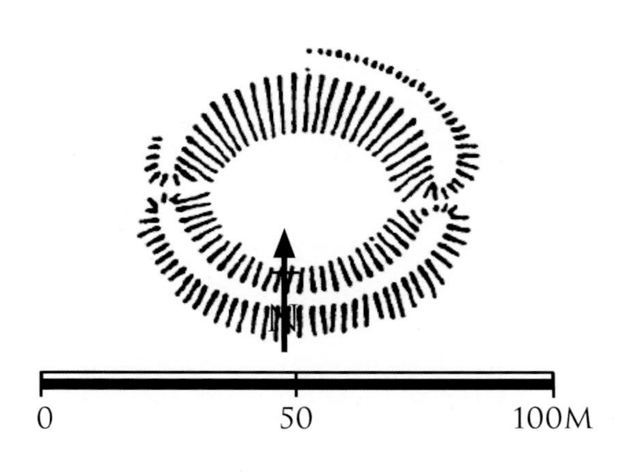

A trial trench dug in 1938 failed to reveal any evidence of an internal ditch. These records were destroyed in 1940, but gave rise to the idea of a post-Roman date. It was thought that the distribution of sherds and flints throughout the earthwork might represent a scraped-up surface yield, normal to an area of intense Romano-British occupation involving lead mines and other industrial activities.**5**

Design and Construction

The date of the construction of the earthwork is at present unknown although, as mentioned above, the presence of several Roman pottery sherds including Samian ware in a seating embankment and on the floor of the monument's east entrance are indicative of a Roman date.

The dimensions of the amphitheatre were about 70m by 61m, with an arena of 32m by 24.4m. **6** The building lay less than 200m to the west of the nearest edge of the settlement. From excavation and aerial photography, it is also almost certain that the structure was a simple Type Ia monument.

The amphitheatre builders' chose a patch of ground sloping from the northwest to the southeast, and burrowed into natural sand to create the arena and then piled the excavated sand around the arena to form the embankments of the *cavea*. However, construction of the arena, which lies 0.47m below the present ground surface, did not yield enough spoil required for the seating banks. To overcome this shortage, the builders used mining waste and also sand obtained from outside the structure to meet the deficit. **7**

Arena, Entrances and Seating

The surfacing material of the arena was sand **8** and the arena was entered via two entrances or *porta pompea.* These entrances would have consisted of passages bounded by seating banks. Compared with other amphitheatres, the passages were quite narrow at a width of 2.5m. **9** Seams of charcoal have been found in the silt which accumulated at the bottom of the western entrance **10,** and possible evidence of palisades which faced the entrance passage walls.

The exact design of the seating arrangements is unknown, but it is reasonable to assume that the amphitheatre could have held a few thousand spectators. The limited scope of the excavations carried out so far means that only the basic characteristics of the *cavea* can be detected. The *cavea* would have been about 18m wide. **11** The seating banks would have stood several metres high to provide a clear view of the arena; the sandy embankment currently stands at a maximum height of 4.5m. **12**

It is likely that the structure did not have a retaining wall and that access to seating may have been via ramps on the rear slopes of the seating banks. Traces of charcoal found on the outer slope of the amphitheatre's north embankment may be vestiges of the building's seating. **13**

Notes

1. NMR Monument Wardens Report ST 45 NE 25.
2. Johnston, D.E., Discovering Roman Britain (2002), 103.
3. Haverford, F., 'The Victorian history of the county of Somerset' 1, in The Victoria history of the counties of England, (1906), 336.
4. Gray, H.St.G., Somerset Archaeology and Natural History: the proceedings, The Somerset Archaeological and Natural History Society 55 (1910), 118-37
5. NMR Monument Wardens Report ST 45 NE 25.
6. Burnham & Wacher, Small Towns of Roman Britain, 209
7. Vatcher, Antiquarian Journal 43 (1963), 197, 199, 206.
8. Moloney, Current Archaeology, 148 (June 1996), 130.
9. Gray, Proceedings of the Somerset Archaeological and Natural History Society 55 (1910), 129, 130-131.
10. ibid., 129.
11. Burham and Wacher, Small Towns of Roman Britain, 209.
12. Gray, Proceedings of the Somerset Archaeological and Natural History Society 55 (1910), 135.
13. ibid., 133.

CHESTER

Chester (*Deva*)
Cheshire

Map ref. SJ 4083 6617

How to get here

The remains of one of the largest and most important amphitheatres in Britain stand on a sandstone bluff overlooking the River Dee; the river that gave the legionary fortress the name Deva. It lies just a short step south-east of the Newgate on the City walls, on the far side of Souter's Lane. However, the Walls were not so extensive in Roman times; the amphitheatre lay just outside the southeast corner of the fortress.

What you can see

The southern half of the amphitheatre is under the grounds of the former Ursuline convent (Dee House). The northern half was excavated and opened to the public in 1972. You can see part of the remains of both phases of the amphitheatre. Phase 1 was an elliptical structure thought to have held about 5,000 to 6,000 spectators.

Phase 2 was also an elliptical structure originally 99m (major axis) north-south by 87.5m (minor axis) east-west. The inner arena wall is estimated to have stood 3.4m high and spectator capacity, still under review, is thought to have been as much as 12,000! Archaeologists have yet to decide if this is indeed the only known example of a Type II ('mini-Imperial') amphitheatre in England and Wales.

The site is open to the public seven days a week, with a purpose-built walkway allowing you to see the excavation.

For further information please contact:
Chester Amphitheatre Project
c/o Chester City Council
The Forum, Chester.
CH12HS

Phone: 01244 402466
e-mail: enquiries@chesteramphitheatre.co.uk
website: www. chesteramphitheatre.co.uk
For general information please phone:
Chester Visitor Centre on 01244 402111.

The Chester amphitheatre project

Although parts of the site have been excavated in the past, there is still much to learn about its history over the last 2,000 years. It is a major element in the city's townscape, yet its environment and presentation is far from ideal.

In order to plan future improvements to the site and its environs, the City Council and English Heritage have joined together to create 'The Chester Amphitheatre Project'. This is a three-year programme of research and investigation, involving excavation, examination of old records, and geophysical and architectural survey.

The first of two excavation seasons took place during the summer of 2004. The archaeological team consisted of professional archaeologists from English Heritage and the City Council, supplemented by students from Liverpool University and Chester College, along with volunteer helpers.

The Amphitheatre Project was set up to explore the archaeological potential of the site and its immediate environs. This will help to formulate future strategies and place the monument within its surrounding landscape.

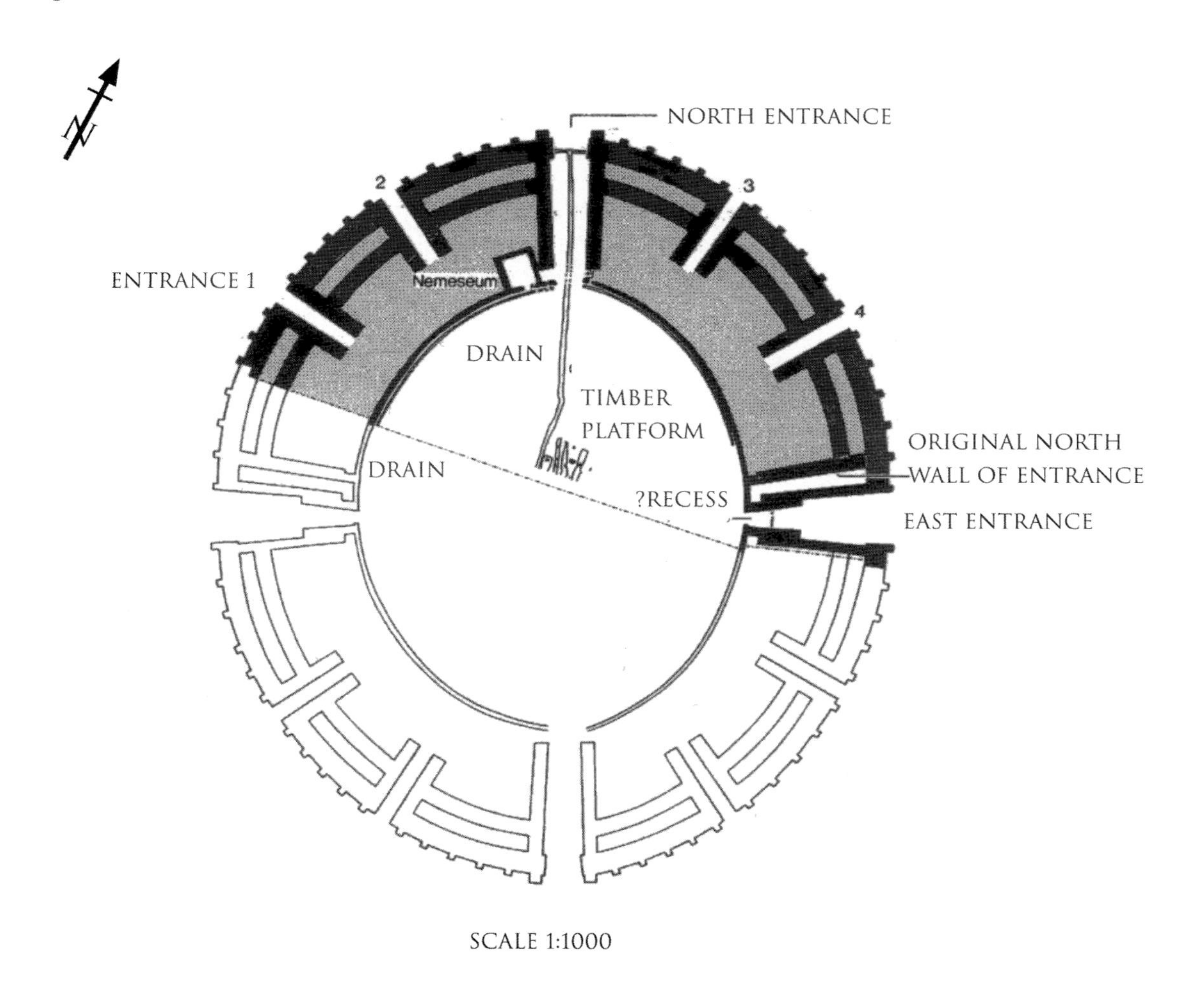

REPRODUCED BY KIND PERMISSION OF
PROFESSOR M.G. FULFORD AND THE SOCIETY
FOR THE PROMORTION OF ROMAN STUDIES

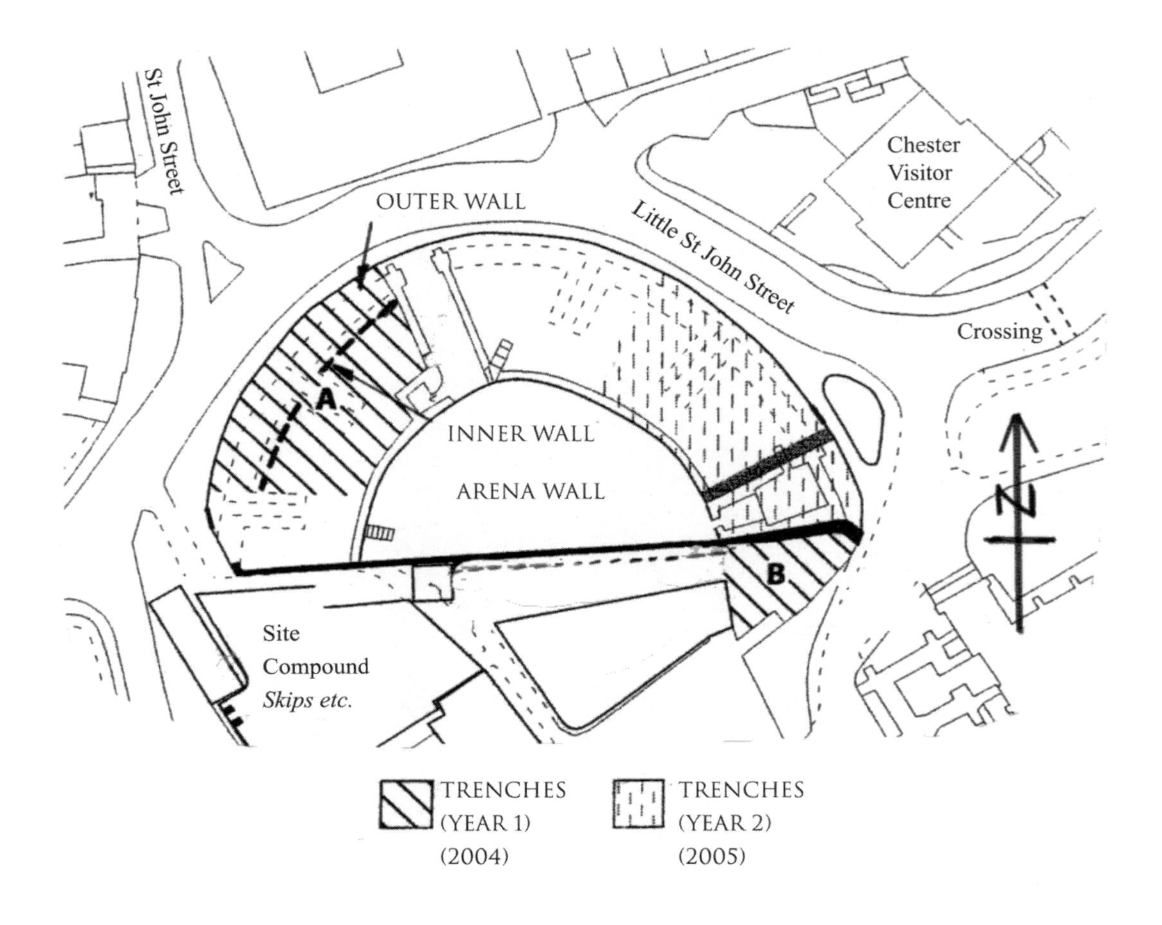

Techniques employed

During the first season's excavation many exciting discoveries have been found using modern archaeological techniques including: geophysical survey (resistivity, magnetometry, and ground penetrating radar), topographical survey, and aerial photography through the use of an unmanned aerial vehicle (a digital camera attached to the bottom of a balloon!). All the results will be integrated and analysed on a Geographic Information System database along with cartographic and pictorial information.

Excavation area A

Located on the north-west side of the amphitheatre, opposite the Newgate, this has been the area where most advances in knowledge have been made. Before excavation began in June 2004 it was not certain what remains had survived, due to two previous archaeological investigations in the 1930s and 1960s and the possibility of cellars associated with buildings still standing on the site until the 1950s.

Fortunately the large 1960s trench occupying the area between the 'concentric wall' and the arena wall had only been partially excavated by F H Thompson.Much of the vital archaeological evidence for ground-level slots for timber beams (interpreted by Thompson as evidence for a timber amphitheatre) had survived for re-examination. Also, the cellars associated with properties on the street frontage were located beneath the modern road and little damage had been done to the remains of the amphitheatre. In fact, other than the previous archaeological investigations, the only real damage inflicted to the amphitheatre during the twentieth century was caused by a network of service trenches to install sewer pipes, manholes and the foundations of a brick garage and car inspection pit.

PHOTO BY MIKE PENNEY

It was soon realised that some time during the later eighteenth or nineteenth centuries a certain amount of ground reduction had taken place, probably in preparation for a programme of new building. This had removed most of the post-Roman stratigraphy from the trench. Consequently, only the deeper features such as cess-pits and wall-robbing trenches remained. Much of 2004 work has concentrated on the excavation and recording of these features.

The trenches dug to rob out stone for other buildings removed large sections of the amphitheatre walls, though the lines of the walls can still be identified. Interestingly, all of the major stone robbing appears to predate the appearance of the medieval cess-pits, though the precise date is still unknown.

It would certainly appear that there were two phases of stone robbing: the first was aimed at the stone of the 'concentric wall' and minor entrances, carefully leaving the outer wall intact and thus suggesting that the latter still had a function. The second phase of stone robbing concentrated on the outer wall, but interestingly the stone robbers were working from the outside of the amphitheatre and seem to have taken care to leave the inner face of the wall intact, again suggesting that it still acted as a sort of boundary.

In one of the public entrances, or *vomitoria,* a massive stone threshold has been found. While the amphitheatre was in use the road around its circumference was constantly re-surfaced. Over time these surfaces spilled over the threshold until the entrance and road combined. After many years of road build-up, a foundation trench was cut to the threshold level and a wall inserted which enclosed the entrance.

The eastern main entrance was also blocked. One of the models for the post-Roman development of the site is that it may have become an independent stronghold. Blocking the entrances would be one way of securing such a place.

Excavation area B

Area B was located in the gardens of Dee House opposite St John's Church. To date, much of the work in this area has been aimed at the excavation and recording of a post-medieval stone building furnished with a full height cellar. This building appears on Hunter's map of 1796 and the backfill of the cellar included pottery of nineteenth-century date. However, the associated stratigraphy suggests that the building is far older than this and its origins may be associated with the monastic enclave known to have existed at St John's prior to the dissolution of the monasteries in the sixteenth century

The over-riding importance of Area B is that unlike Area A, post-Roman stratigraphy is clearly intact and a full archaeological sequence from the first to the twentieth century should ultimately be recovered from the 2005 excavations.

2004 artefacts

Thousands of artefacts have been recovered from an excavation of this size, all needing to be cleaned, sorted, catalogued, packaged and analysed. The artefacts found ranged from early Roman pottery and brooches, civil war buckles and musket balls to a worn-out shovel blade left behind by the 1960s excavators!

In the early stages of the dig most of the finds were from the topsoil or the backfill of the earlier excavations. However, they are now helping to provide some interesting information about the history of the site. A large group of seventeenth and eighteenth-century pottery from Area B appears to be the result of rubbish dumping. Amongst the eighteenth-century pottery are pieces of attractive, good quality tablewares, including fine white stoneware plates and tin-glazed ware painted with Chinese style patterns, possibly made in Liverpool. The quality of the pottery suggests that some of it came from a prosperous household. Some very interesting medieval finds have also come to light such as a copper-alloy pen and a seal matrix.

AMPHITHEATRE EXCAVATION 2004 - VIEWED FROM THE NORTH
NORTH ENTRANCE AND EXCAVATION AREA A

PHOTO BY MIKE PENNEY

Roman items unearthed during the dig include:
A copper alloy brooch originally decorated with coloured enamel, its geometric pattern of triangles was popular on items such as dress fasteners or brooches in the 1st and 2nd centuries AD.

A Samian ware bowl made in Gaul at the end of the 1st or beginning of the 2nd century AD. It shows two gladiators and two small cupids above a dolphin. Finding this artefact at the amphitheatre and the use of gladiators and cupids could mean that the bowl was intended for a ritual function. Cupid gladiators are associated with the cult of the goddess Venus. **1**

One of the most exciting finds unearthed was part of a Roman sword handle, the type carried by legionaries. Though the fact that it was discovered in the amphitheatre may suggest other exciting possibilities.

Future work

A second season of excavation will be carried out in the summer of 2005. The sections exposed by digging out the wall robbing trenches have given tantalising previews of the complex Roman archaeology still to be excavated in 2005. **2**

History of the site

It used to be believed that the amphitheatre was built in the 70s AD, by Legion II Adiutrix. However, the excavations carried out since the year 2000 have revealed another building underneath the east entrance, which suggests that there was a Roman building here before the amphitheatre. It is not known yet what it was, as so little evidence has been found. So the monument may have been built later than the 70s, but still in the first century.

It is believed that sometime before the middle of the 2nd century, the amphitheatre stopped being used. It may only have seen service for 20 or 30 years. The arena became a rubbish dump and the building slowly fell into disrepair.

It was brought back into use some time after the 270s, but only for a short time. The staircases up to the seats were repaired, a new surface was laid in the arena and the east entrance was drastically remodelled. The current theory is that the amphitheatre was brought back into service for a very special reason.

In AD 287 the province of Britain revolted from the Roman Empire, and was not reconquered until 296/7. It is known that one of the British legions was a strong supporter of the rebel governor, Marcus Aurelius Carausius. Perhaps the rebel legion was Chester's XX Valeria Victrix? The victorious government forces may have rebuilt the amphitheatre, always a potent

RELIEF OF A RETIARIUS (GLADIATOR) FOUND NEAR TO THE AMPHITHEATRE IN THE 18TH CENTURY

REPRODUCED BY PERMISSION OF SAFFRON WALDEN MUSEUM

THE EASTERN ENTRANCE WITH SMALL CHAMBER WITH REMAINS OF STEPS

PHOTO BY MIKE PENNEY

symbol of Rome power, as a place of very public execution for the ringleaders, with the remainder of the disgraced legion and local dignitaries forced to watch in terror!

By the beginning of the fourth century it is believed that the refurbished amphitheatre had fallen into decay and the site began to be used for other purposes. Two lean-to buildings against the arena wall were found during the 1960s, and postholes found in the middle of the arena could be the remains of a sub-Roman hall building.

A feature of the eastern entrance of the amphitheatre is a number of very large sandstone blocks, together with the remains of steps on the south side. The masonry is said to be unlike any other Roman work in Chester, and the wear on the steps implies centuries of use. One suggestion is that the old entrance passage was converted in the Dark Ages into a crypt for an early version of St John's Church.

By about 1200, people were living on the site, perhaps in the dilapidated shell of the Roman building. The area was cleared during the Civil War siege of Chester in the 1640s. Later two large Georgian houses, built in the 1730s, dominated the site. One was St John's House, which was demolished in order that the northern half of the amphitheatre could be excavated; the other is Dee House, which still stands over part of the southern half of the site.

Design & Construction

Currently there are two theories about how the amphitheatre was built:

Theory a) The amphitheatre was constructed completely from timber, and some time later rebuilt in stone.

Theory b) The amphitheatre was made from a mixture of wood and stone, with timber staging to support the front rows of seats.

Whichever theory is the correct one, there is still a large amount of information already known about the design and layout of the amphitheatre from the 1960s excavation:

The 1960s excavations – What Thomson discovered

A stone wall surrounded the arena and the higher outer wall was also of stone, but more massively built. This was to hold the mass of earth, sloping inwards to the arena, on which the seating, perhaps of wood, was placed. The entrances were also built in stone.

Even during the preliminary excavation of 1960 traces of an earlier amphitheatre were found, and later excavation made it possible to recover much of the plan.

The arena was apparently the same size for both structures, 58m on the long and 49m on the short axis. The earlier seating was, however, much less capacious: it was based on a grid of massive horizontal beams, set 1.8m apart at their outer ends where they were linked by a system of lateral beams, and converging as they ran inwards where they were again linked by lateral beams. The whole served as a rigid foundation into which were mortised equally massive uprights at approximately I.5m intervals; these, presumably strengthened by cross-bracing, would have formed the frame-work for planked seats rising in tiers from the edge of the arena. It is thought that the first amphitheatre was built at the latter part of the 1st century.

Although the arena remained at its original size, the opportunity was later taken to excavate it down to the surface of the natural sandstone, both to provide material for the seating bank and also to reduce the structural height of the amphitheatre above the existing ground level. At the edges the vertical sandstone-face was revetted with a mortared stone wall which continued upwards to a total height of perhaps 3.7m, forming a parapet to the gangway immediately behind it. This arena wall was normally 0.6m thick, but occasionally nearer 0.9m, and was capped with a semi-circular coping; the face fronting the arena still retained substantial traces of a plaster rendering which had apparently been colour-washed for decorative effect.

The space devoted to seating was now widened to about 15m and at the outer edge was built a massive mortared stone wall 2.7m thick where it passed down into the foundations but probably reduced to about 2.1m in the upper courses. Externally it was provided with massive buttresses, 0.9m square and probably 3.7m apart, centre to centre. Between the arena and outer walls was piled the earth derived from the excavation of the arena, sloping upwards and outwards to act as the base for the rows of seats.

At the northern end of the arena (and presumably at the south end too, though this has still to be excavated) was a passage with side-walls built in stone, running from the arena to the exterior of the amphitheatre. It was 3.4m wide at the arena end, where it could be blocked by a two-leaved wooden gate, opening inwards, and gradually widened to 5.5m at its outer end. The passage floor sloped downwards to the arena and there was probably a vaulted roof; at the arena end flights of steps led left and right, immediately behind the leaves of the gate, to give access to the gangway behind the arena wall.

EASTERN ENTRANCE "CONVERGING" TO ARENA

PHOTO BY MIKE PENNEY

At the east end of the arena, on its short axis, was another entrance but this did not communicate directly with the arena. At the outer end there was a break of 7.3m in the outer wall from which a level paved surface led inwards, bounded by side walls which gradually converged. At 11m from the outer face of the amphitheatre they were within 5m of each other and at this point flights of steps 0.9m wide ran upwards against the sides of the passage to reach the gangway behind the arena wall.

Meanwhile, the passage continued for a further 3.7m down a shallow flight of stairs to enter a small room 3m long by 2.4m and 1.8m wide at its east and west ends respectively. At the west end, an entrance nearly 1.2m wide, which could be closed by an inward-opening door, led into the arena. There was no clue to the purpose of this small chamber. Immediately over it, however, it seems probable that there was a fairly elaborate structure serving as a 'box' for the senior officers of the legion, with a tiled roof supported on stone columns and perhaps even glazed windows. Whether a similar sequence of structures existed on the west side of the arena is not yet known, as this lies outside the boundary of the excavated area; but there probably was, even if the arrangement was not precisely the same.

In each quadrant between the four suggested entrances of importance at the ends of the long and short axes excavation suggests that there were two minor entrances, defined by stone side walls, running inwards for about 10m. Through them flights of stone steps, 1.8m wide, led upwards to emerge slightly

THE NEMESEUM PHOTO BY MIKE PENNEY

over half-way down the seating-bank to which they were clearly intended to give access for the bulk of the audience. Thus, for the amphitheatre as a whole there would appear to have been a total of twelve entrances of differing degrees of importance.

A notable feature of the amphitheatre was a small room immediately west of the northern main entrance that served as a shrine of the goddess *Nemesis,* who was particularly venerated by gladiators. A door 1.5m wide led through the arena wall into a small room, 4.3m by 3.7m, concealed within the seating bank. It had a boarded floor and plastered walls, while along the west wall ran a narrow stone bench. However, the important feature was a stone altar, originally on a sandstone plinth at the rear centre, dedicated to the goddess *Nemesis* by the centurion Sextius Marcianus as "*the result of a vision.*"

Certain features of interest were observed during the clearance of the arena. In the centre, three parallel lines of post-holes suggested that a wooden platform stood there, perhaps to serve as a dais for ceremonial purposes. The arena itself was apparently surfaced with stone slabs, although few of these survived.

Drainage must always have been a problem for a hollowed-out area standing below general ground level. In front of the arena wall was a gutter to take seepage from the mass of the seating bank. In addition an axial gutter ran under the floor of the northern main entrance and across the arena, diverging from this line to avoid the timber platform but presumably resuming the original line so as to pass through the southern main entrance and so into the River Dee. All these drains were of the type known as 'rumble' drains and were cut into the rock or lined with stone slabs to the width of 305mm, half-filled with sand, and then topped with stone slabs to the surrounding level. Drainage was by gradual seepage rather than by an unimpeded flow.

The axial drain was combined with another feature in the arena. At a slightly higher level two parallel lines of sandstone blocks, varying from 1.2m to 1.5m apart, acted as kerbs to a sand and rubble pathway. This continued in a straight line beyond the point where the underlying drain diverged to avoid the central platform, and the assumption must be that it was the ceremonial approach to the platform itself, along which legionaries would march to present themselves on formal occasions.

The amphitheatre did not remain structurally unchanged throughout the Roman occupation of Chester. The clearest evidence for this was the accumulation of a layer of soil, 305mm to 457mm thick, on the original arena floor, a layer which contained a fair number of third-century coins to approximately AD 270. It would appear that the amphitheatre was out of use for a time during the third century, but then a new slabbed floor was laid at a higher level. This in turn involved certain changes in the *Nemeseum* - the narrowing of the door, the insertion of a new sill and stone floor, and the installation of two column bases perhaps to serve as the bases for cult images. There may have been other changes, for instance in the entrances, but the evidence was obscured by the collapse of roofs, when the amphitheatre finally fell into disuse, a process that (Thompson conjectured) began about AD 350 on the evidence of the pottery sealed beneath the tumbled masonry. 3

Notes

1. Bignor Roman Villa guidebook, 15 and rear cover.
2. Garner, D. & Dunn, G., 'Gladiators at the amphitheatre' The Past Uncovered, newsletter of Chester Archaeology (October 2004), 1-2.
3. Thompson, F.H., Roman Amphitheatre Chester (1977), 2-5

Postscript:

In May 2005 the BBC Two 'Timewatch' programme, 'Britain's Lost Colosseum', featured the 2004 excavation of Chester Amphitheatre. From these excavations three major points have emerged:

a) There were two amphitheatres, the first being much smaller than the second.

b) The first amphitheatre was constructed of stone with a timber seating arrangement, and not an all timber structure as previously thought. The second amphitheatre was also constructed of stone, but was a much larger and grander building.

c) Sadly, no evidence has yet come to light to specifically date both structures.

CHICHESTER

Chichester (*Noviomagus Reginorum*)

Map ref: SU 8663 0466

West Sussex

How to get here

The site of the amphitheatre can be reached by walking out of Eastgate along the 'Hornet' and turning right down a narrow passageway or 'twitten' which forms the north end of Whyke Lane (this might well have been the route in Roman times as well). **1**

Museum and Tourist information

Chichester District Museum covers the history, archaeology, and geology of Chichester and the surrounding area through displays, hands-on activities and changing exhibitions. Find out about Boxgrove man, the Roman city of *Noviomagus*, and Georgian Chichester. The Museum also looks after the Guildhall in Priory Park. For further information contact:

Chichester District Museum
Chichester
West Sussex
PO19 1PB
T: 01243 784683
F: 01243 776766
E: districtmuseum@chichester.gov.uk
www.chichester.gov.uk/museum

TIC T: 01243 775888

What you can see

The amphitheatre lies outside the Roman City of Chichester and is visible as an earthwork or sub-circular bank 1.7m high by about 115m in overall diameter with an interior depth of 1.8m. The bank is complete except where it has been destroyed by housing development on the south-west side. **2**

Site History & Design Features

Trial excavations in 1935 showed that the amphitheatre was elliptical in plan with the long axis about 57m and the short axis about 46m. The floor of the arena has been excavated to a depth of 1.25m below Roman ground level and a bank constructed around it that would have held seating for spectators. This bank was revetted on the inside by a wall about 1.23m wide. From the very sparse dating evidence, the excavator, G. M. White, concluded that the amphitheatre was built between AD 70-80 and went out of use by the end of the second century, with the revetting wall being robbed for building stone soon afterwards. **3**

G. M. White's conclusions are now treated with some caution, because these were no more than trial excavations and only a small sample of dateable evidence was recovered. However, it is likely that a date of AD 70 is about right for the construction, but more excavation would be required before a date of the late second century can be accepted for its abandonment **4**

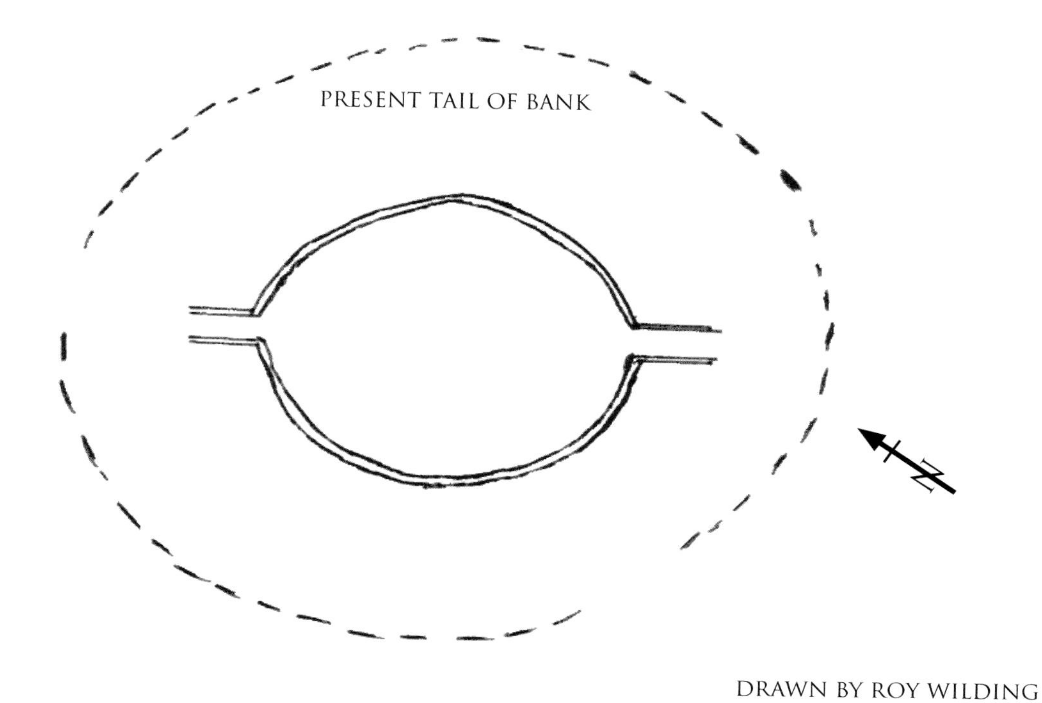

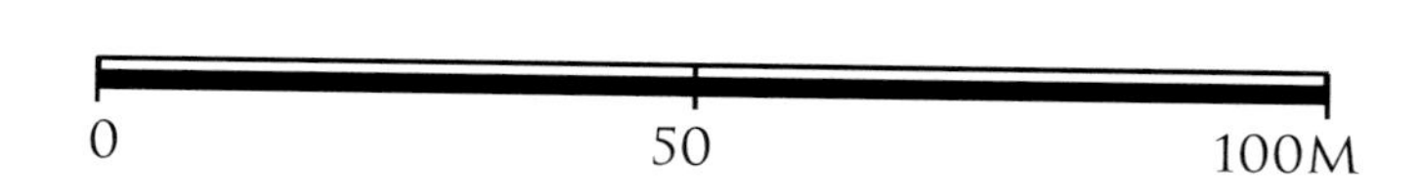

Wacher states that several amphitheatres in Britain are outside the walls of towns and that there is no reason *per se* why the amphitheatre at Chichester should have been robbed of stone for the construction of the town defences in the 3rd century. The implication being that occupation/use may have lasted longer that White suggests. **5**

Notes

1. A. Down, Roman Chichester (1988), 51-52
2. NMR Monument Wardens Report SU 80 Se 103 (2004);
   NMR Investigators Comments FI PASS 22-Sep –1972.
3. G. M. White, The Antiquaries Journal: journal of the Society of Antiquaries of London 16 (1936), 149-159.
4. A. Down, Roman Chichester, 51.
5. J. S. Wacher, The Towns of Roman Britain (1975), 248.

CIRENCESTER

Cirencester (*Corinium Dobunnorum*) Gloucestershire

Map ref: SP0201 0141

How to get here

Access to the amphitheatre is free of charge and its entrance is situated in Cotswold Avenue, on the south side of the town. Parking at the site is fairly limited, and if visitors decide to travel by car, they are asked to respect the residents of the area by parking considerately. The nearest car parks are within ten minutes walk from the amphitheatre. Sadly, due to the nature of the site, there is very limited wheelchair access.

Museum and Tourist information

Corinium Museum is one of the finest in Britain: two years and over £5 million in the making, the Museum has been transformed into a must-see visitor attraction of the Cotswolds. For further information contact:

Corinium Museum
Park Street
Cirencester
Gloucestershire
GL7 2BX
T: 01285 655611
E: museum@cotswold.gov.uk
WWW.cotswold.gov.uk

TIC T: 01285 654180

What you can see

Situated to the southwest of the Roman town walls, on the probable line of the Fosse Way, the Roman amphitheatre survives as an oval earthwork with the arena entrances clearly visible. **1**

Site History & Design Features

The amphitheatre was built during the early second century AD within an earlier Roman quarry. It had an oval plan with the central arena measuring 49m by 41m. The arena floor had a sand and fine gravel surface. Earthen banks enclosed it with an entrance at either end of its long axis. The seating banks were up to 30m wide and retained by timber and drystone walls. Each bank consisted of a series of shallow terraces, retained by a drystone wall, which may have carried seats of wooden planks.

The building was later reinforced with masonry walls and the outer 21m of the entrance passages were vaulted to provide additional seating. By the later second century the arena was rebuilt and a small chamber flanking each entrance to the arena was added. (See plan of amphitheatre) It is not certain what the purpose of these chambers was, although they may have been used as prisons or cages for holding criminals or wild animals. One of the rooms may also have contained a shrine.

Excavations, which took place in the 19th century and in the 1960s, indicate that the amphitheatre was out of use by the third or early fourth century when the north-eastern entrance was demolished and metalled surfaces laid. It is possible that by this time the amphitheatre may have been the site of an extra-mural market.

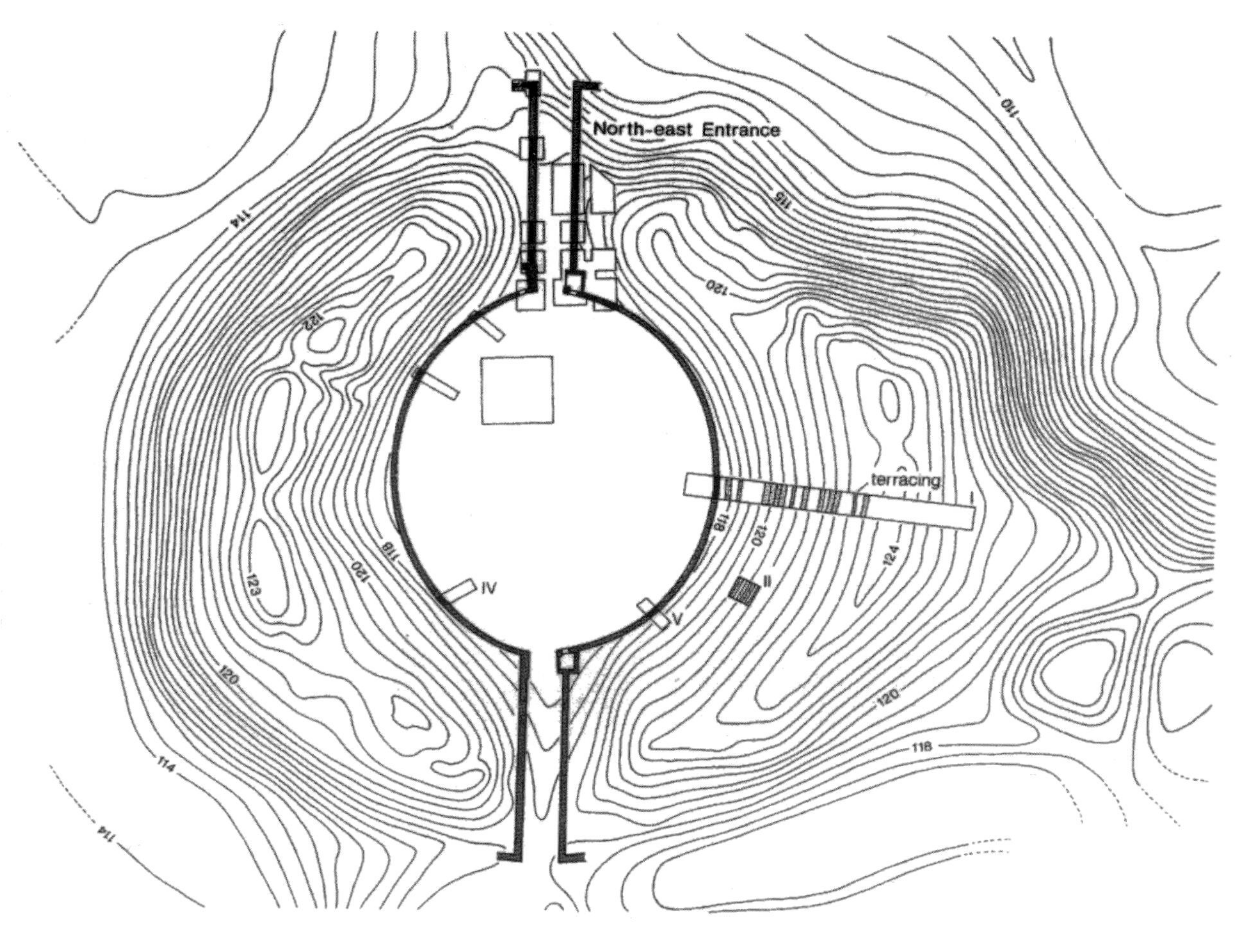

SCALE, 1:1000

In the fifth century there was further activity which included the restoration of the amphitheatre entrance, additional street metalling and construction of a large timber building within the arena. Outside the arena quarrying also took place, and it is possible that one of the quarry ditches may have been used for defensive purposes, the theory being that the amphitheatre was used as a fortified retreat. The amphitheatre area's still popular local name is the 'Bull Ring' and may indicate a later use for the site. **2**

EXCAVATED BANK

IMAGES REPRODUCED BY KIND PERMISSION OF PROFESSOR M.G. FULFORD AND THE SOCIETY FOR THE PROMORTION OF ROMAN STUDIES

Important Roman Artefacts Found

A. 'Bird-Brooch' found during excavations at the amphitheatre
B. Leopard from the Orpheus Mosaic – Corinium Museum

A. "BIRD BROOCH"

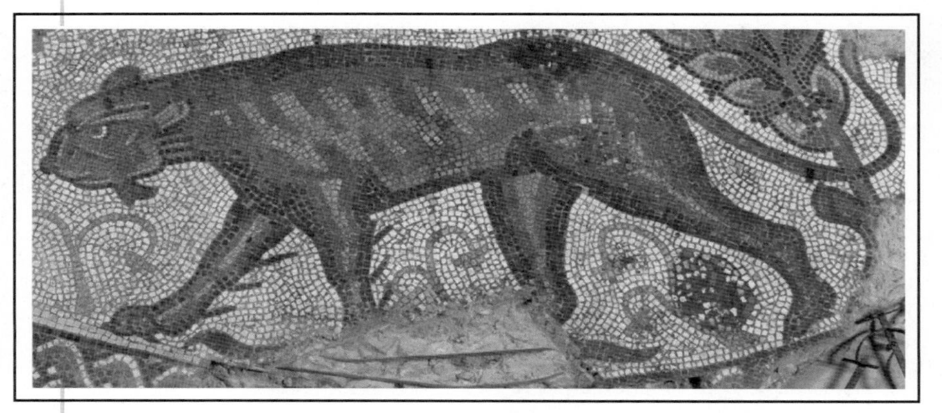

B. LEOPARD FROM THE ORPHEUS MOSAIC - CORINIUM MUSEUM

Notes

1. NMR Monument Wardens Report SP 00 SW 110
2. J. Wacher, The Towns of Roman Britain (1995), 307-8,322; J. S. Wacher, Cirencester Roman amphitheatre (1981); The Antiquaries Journal; journal of the Society of Antiquaries of London 43 (1963), 23-26; *Ibid.*, 44 (1964), 17-18; *Ibid.*, 47 (1967), 185-188.

DORCHESTER

Dorchester (*Durnovaria*) Maumbury Rings

Map ref: SY 6902 8992

How to get here

The amphitheatre is in Dorchester itself, on the junction of Maumbury Road and Weymouth Avenue. It is sandwiched between two railway tracks, and very near to Dorchester's railway station 'south' and railway station 'west'. There are several public car parks in close proximity to the site.

Museums and Tourist information

Dorset County Museum
High Street West
Dorchester
DT1 1XA

T: 01305 262735
www.dorsetcountymuseum.org.

TIC T: 01395 267992

What you can see

The grass-covered sub-circular earthwork enclosure is in a good state of preservation though the summit of the bank, average width 4.0m, has been damaged in several places. The side of the bank is steep and the interior has been damaged on the east and west sides by a narrow terrace that gives a broken-slope effect. In the east the average vertical drop internally is 5.6m and externally 4.0m.

From the centre of the interior of the amphitheatre the land slopes gradually up to the only remaining entrance in the northeast. There is generally a fairly steep slope to the top of the bank. However, a Civil War gun platform and ramp on the monument has slightly lowered the height of the bank, and made the ascent in the southwest more gradual than elsewhere. There is now no trace of either an internal or external ditch. **1**

The long axis of the amphitheatre runs 17-20 degrees east of north. **2**

Site History

Today the amphitheatre has an internal diameter of about 47m. However it is thought that the original size of the arena was 59m by 53m, with an external amphitheatre diameter of 101m. A large stone was discovered, during cultivation in 1849, to the west of the northeast entrance; it was reburied but no trace of it was found in subsequent excavations. Some excavation work was carried out on the site in 1879, but the principal excavations were those undertaken by Harold St George Gray between 1908 and 1913.

These excavations showed the site to have originated in the later Neolithic period, although there is some evidence for pre-henge features. The site was discovered to have comprised of an external bank with an internal ditch, the latter actually comprising of a series of deep shafts cut into the chalk. There were up to 45 shafts, up to 11m deep. In these shafts were various deposits of artefacts and other material including; antler, animal and human bone, flints and carved chalk, including a phallic object. It appears that these shafts or pits may have been deliberately backfilled.

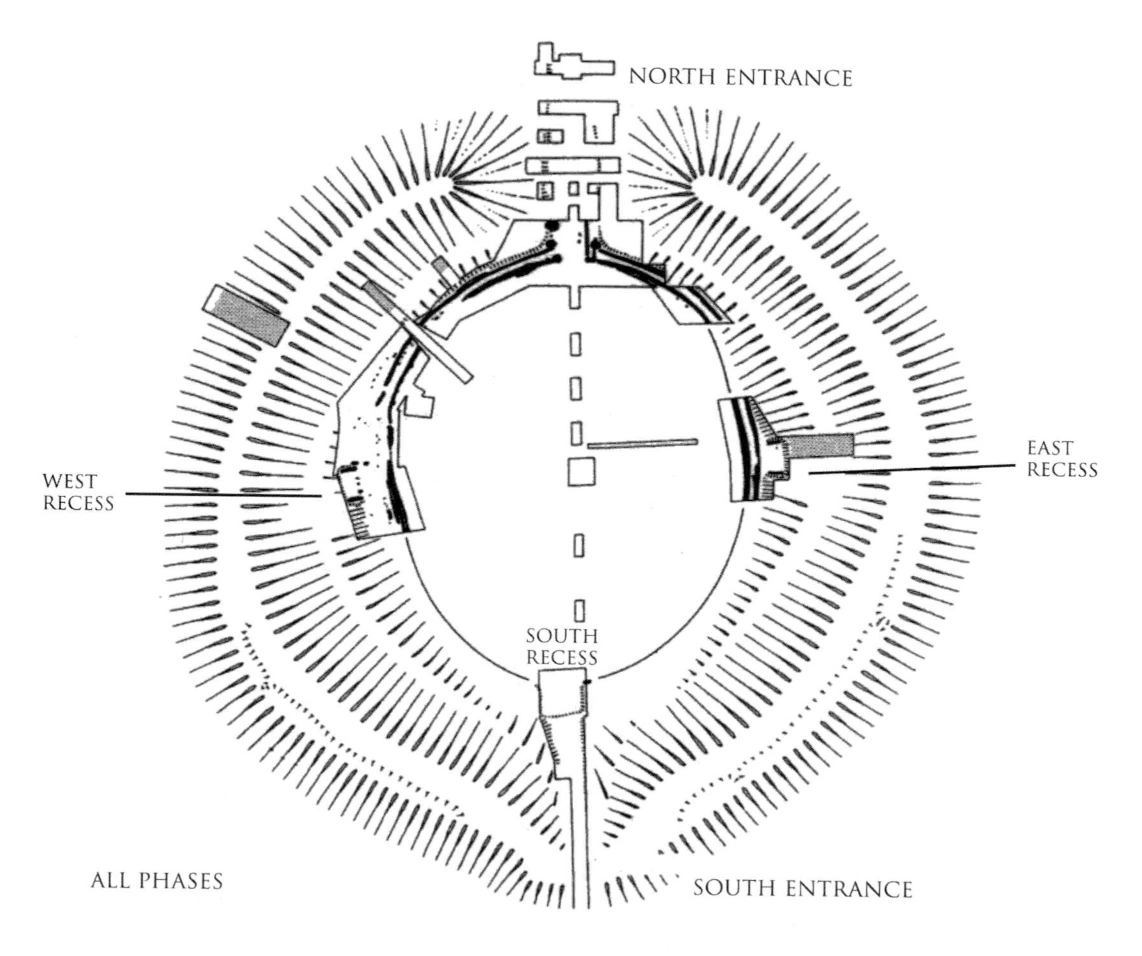

SCALE 1:1000

REPRODUCED BY KIND PERMISSION OF PROFESSOR M.G. FULFORD AND THE SOCIETY FOR THE PROMORTION OF ROMAN STUDIES

OUTLINE RECONSTRUCTION OF THE ORIGINAL ROMAN LAYOUT (RECESS TO LEFT AND POST TRENCHES TO RIGHT)

Dating evidence was sparse, but comprised of a single Grooved Ware sherd from one pit, and a Beaker sherd from a secondary fill material. Two antler picks recovered by Gray have since been radiocarbon dated. They produced uncalibrated determinations of 1690+/-70 BC and 1700+/-70 BC. The henge had a single entrance to the northeast. **3**

PREHISTORIC SHAFTS (a)

Design & Construction

The site was substantially modified in the Roman period when it was adapted as an amphitheatre. A date suggested for the building of the structure is in the Claudio-Neronian period (AD 41-68). **4** Whatever the precise date, it is clear that the amphitheatre was built before the last quarter of the first century. It was located 800m outside the south gate of the Roman town **5** and was a Type Ia structure, built entirely of timber and earth. **6**

The designers of the amphitheatre took advantage of the artificial feature of the existing Neolithic henge to form the basic structure of the amphitheatre. The chalk-cut Henge offered the builders an area enclosed by a roughly circular earthwork pierced by a single entrance in the north. **7**

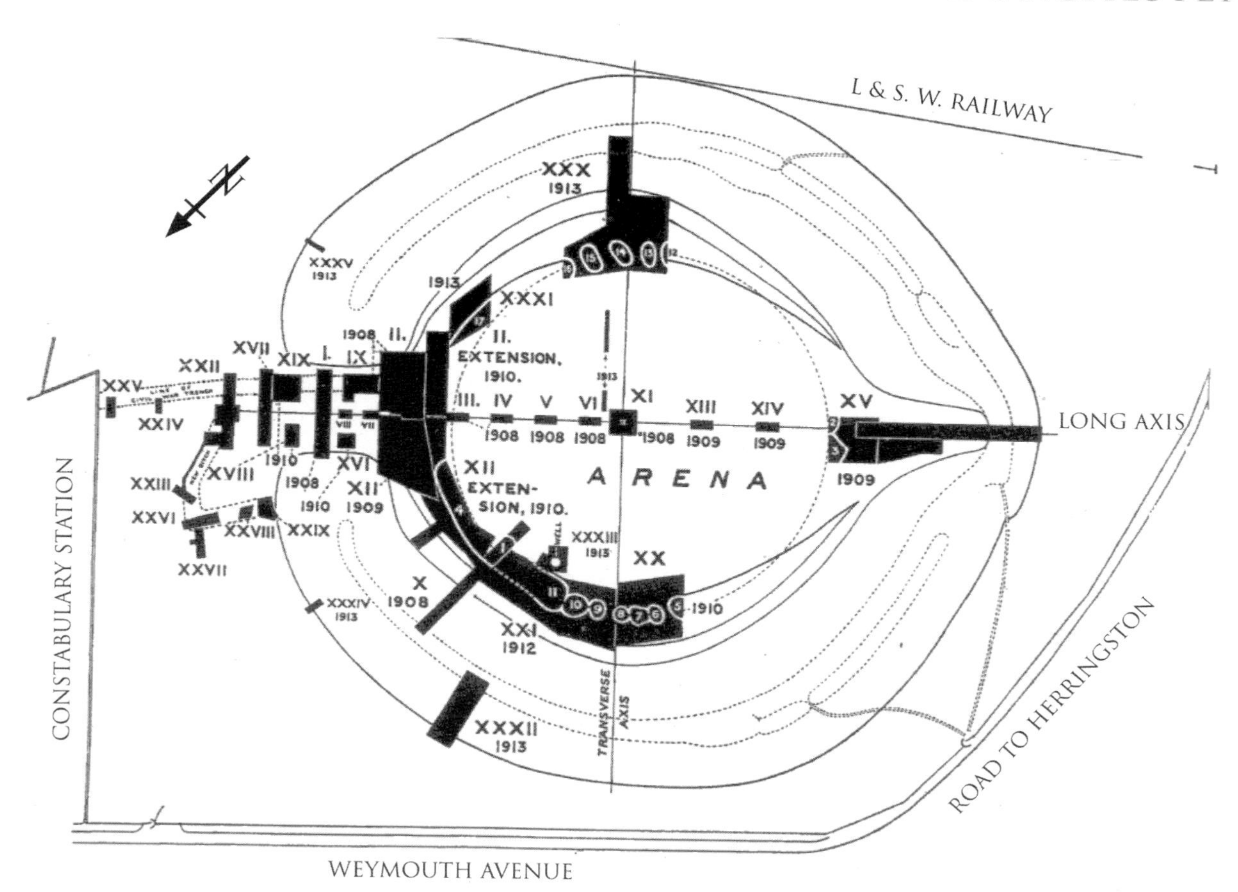

SKETCH PLAN OF THE AMPHITHEATRE SHOWING THE POSITION AND EXTENT OF THE CUTTINGS 1908 - 1913 (b)

WALLING ENCLOSURE, SHAFTS ETC (c)

It was relatively easy to convert the henge into an amphitheatre by excavating the arena from the chalk floor of the enclosure to a depth of 3.0m. The internal ditch was destroyed together with the 45 Neolithic shafts, and the chalk rubble was dumped from the excavated arena onto the already existing bank. **8**

MARGIN OF ARENA AND SHAFT ON THE NORTH (d)

Arena

Gravel appears to have been the surfacing material of the arena. **9** The arena also appears to have been equipped with a shallow axial gully which survives partially in front of the building's north *porta pompea.* **10**

Evidence of the arena timber revetment walls, of the building's initial phase, has survived in the form of post-holes and imprints. A distinctive feature of this amphitheatre is that two concentric timber walls surrounded the arena. An outer wall served to revet the chalk face, exposed by lowering the arena, and support the rubble bank forming the auditorium and an inner wall which demarcated the arena. **11**

The outer (revetment wall) trench was composed of straight segments and was packed with chalk rubble. The arrangement of uprights in straight segments suggests that the posts of each section were connected by horizontal tie beams. The resulting framework of posts and beams, which would have had to be at least 4.6m high to reach beyond the top of the chalk face, seems to have been sheathed with vertical planking. **12**

It has been conjectured that the 0.61 to 0.91 wide space between the inner and outer walls may have served as a service corridor, as it was accessible through breaks between the arena wall and the inner palisade at the north *portae pompae*. **13** It has also been suggested that the inner wall may have been a safety barrier, consisting of posts supporting strong netting or palisading, to protect the crowd from the escape of wild animals. **14** (See section on amphitheatre design features).

Chambers

There were two chambers sited at each end of the arena's short axis, which were accessible only from the arena. The lack of exterior access to these chambers may imply that they were not used as beast pens, but may have been used as shrines or performers' waiting rooms and for storage. **15**

The two short axis chambers were hollowed out of the chalk face surrounding the arena when the builders converted the henge into an amphitheatre. The chambers measured over 3.0m in length, narrowing in width from about 6.0m at the rear to 4.0 at the front. Evidence suggests that the chambers were lined with timber walling.

Further evidence that the chambers may have served a cult purpose is that one of the east alcove's sidewalls and both of the west alcove's wall featured chalk-cut niches; which may have housed effigies of a god or goddess. The absence of an additional entrance at the rear of the chambers is considered proof that they were not used as *carceres* (animal pens).
The amphitheatre also had a third chamber which lay at the southern end of the building's long axis, on the location of what was to later become the building's southern *porta pompae*. Its purpose is unknown because the southern entrance later overlay it. However, it is clear that the room was rectangular and about 4.3m in length by 6.7m in width. **16**

Entrances

Although amphitheatres were typically provided with a *porta pompae* at each end of the long axis, Dorchester's only had one in its initial phase. It lay at the north end of the long axis on the location or the existing gap in the Neolithic earthwork. Later, the southern chamber was replaced by a second *porta pompea.* **17** Another interesting feature of this building is that the entrances appear to have been devoid of a wall screening the exposed chalk banks. The *porta pompae* were unroofed and about 4.3m wide. **18**

Seating

The apparent lack of a rear revetment wall may indicate that only the inward slope of the banks, not their full width, could have supported seating. **19**
The apparent lack of internal access to the seating banks may indicate that spectators reached their places from the rear of the embankment. **20**

Roman artefacts found

Finds are held in Dorchester County Museum

Notes

1. NMR Monument Wardens Report SY 68 NE 2
2. Fulford, 'The Silchester Amphitheatre; excavations of 1979-85' in Britannia monograph series 10 (1989), 179
3. Antiquity, Antiquity Publications Limited, 13 (1939), 155-8; Proceedings of the Dorset Natural History and Antiquarian Field Club 7, (1885), Pope, A, 'The amphitheatre at Dorset', 66-9:
   Ibid., 29 (1908), Gray, H St G, 'Interim report on the excavations at Maumbury Rings, Dorchester', 256-72;
   Ibid., 30 (1909), 215-35;
   Ibid., 31 (1910), 'Short report on the excavations of Maumbury Rings of 1910', 232-66;
   Ibid., 34 (1913), 80-106;
4. Bradley, R, 'Maumbury Rings, Dorchester: The Excavations of 1908-1913',
   Archaeologia 105 (1976), 73-74.
5. Fulford, M. 'Silchester Amphitheatre' AntiquarianJournal 65 (1985), 39.
6. Golvin, L'Amphitheatre romain, 76, 86, 87, 88.
7. Bradley, Archaeologia 105 (1976), 91
8. Ibid., 38
9. Bradley, Archaeologia 105 (1976), 38.
10. Ibid., 42, 51, 54.
11. Ibid., 46
12. Ibid., 43, 45, 47
13. Ibid., 53.
14. Ibid., 53
15. Fulford, Silchester Amphitheatre, 181.
16. Bradley, Archaeologia, 49.
17. Ibid., 52, 58, 74
18. Ibid., 49.
19. Bradley Archaeologia 105 (1976), 156.
20. Ibid., 105, 52, 6.

Diagrams a-d source: The proceedings of the Dorset Natural History and Historical Society 1908-1914- Maumbury Rings Dorchester; 7; 29; 30; 31; 34 and 35

FORDEN GAER

Forden Gaer
Montgomershire, Wales

Map ref: SO 2104 9908

How to get here

The site is in the community of Forden on private farmland.

What you can see

The cropmark complex occupies a low hollow and consists of nested subcircular features, about 24m, 50m and 76m across, with an approach way from the south. **1**

Site History

Forden Gaer was the site of a Roman auxiliary fort that occupied a key position in the central Marches of Wales on the eastern bank of the River Severn, immediately to the north of the historic ford of Rhydwhiman. According to Crew, the complex is reminiscent of that at Tomen-Y-Mur, Meirionnydd **2** (See Tomen-Y-Mur).

The complex is suggested to represent a *ludus*, or military arena/amphitheatre associated with a Roman military settlement, somewhat similar to the gyrus at the Lunt **3 (**See Baginton). It seems probable that the fort may have been occupied from the Flavian period up until the fourth century. **4**
However, the precise history and period for the amphitheatre is at present unclear.

Notes

1. Cadw Monument Wardens Report unnumbered
2. Crew. P., ' Forden Gaer, Montgomery', Archaeology and Art', BBCS 28.4., 730.
3. *Ibid.*, 741.
4. *Ibid.*, 741.

FRILFORD

Frilford
Vale of White Horse
Oxfordshire

Map ref: SU 441 963

How to get here

At the junction of the River Ock and Roman Road (A338), in the parish of Marcham.

What you can see

Aerial photographs indicate a possible amphitheatre at the bottom of a dry shallow valley running southward towards the River Ock. **1**

Site History & Design Features

In 1981 a trench was cut across the bank and down into the arena, and another investigated a small rectangular chamber to the south. The first trench uncovered the bank of an amphitheatre, which was of clay and rubble. There was a 1.0m wide mortared stone wall, still standing to a height of 0.4m, on the arena side to a possible floor at 1.5m below ground level. It is thought that this wall was preceded by one of timber belonging to the amphitheatre's timber phase, whose vestiges were revealed in the cross-section of the bank. **2** No evidence has yet been found of an external wall supporting the *cavea.* **3**

The structure is thought to be a Type Ia amphitheatre of about 67-69m overall. In size its arena was approximately 45m in diameter, and had been lowered to provide material for a surrounding earth bank 11 to 14m wide. Aerial photos indicated entrances on the west and possibly on the east, with a small rectangular walled alcove in the bank to the south. **4**

This chamber is located at the southern end of the secondary axis. It communicated only with the arena. It was a rectangular recess built into the earth bank and lined with walls constructed in the same way as the arena wall. Excavations revealed a roughly rectangular mass of stone, possibly the remains of an altar plinth, in the centre of the floor. This room is thought to have been a *Nemeseum* or an animal holding pen. **5** The amphitheatre may have been furnished with a tribunals or boxes at each end of its short axis; the existence of the alcove at the south end of the secondary axis could imply that it once supported a raised structure of some kind, perhaps a *tribunalia* or box. **6**

The discovery of the amphitheatre 200m east of the temple suggests that the temple complex represented a major religious centre in the Roman period. **7.**

Finds

Roman pottery, animal bones and late 3rd century Roman coins were found. **8**

Notes

1. NMR Monument Wardens Report SU 49 NW 41

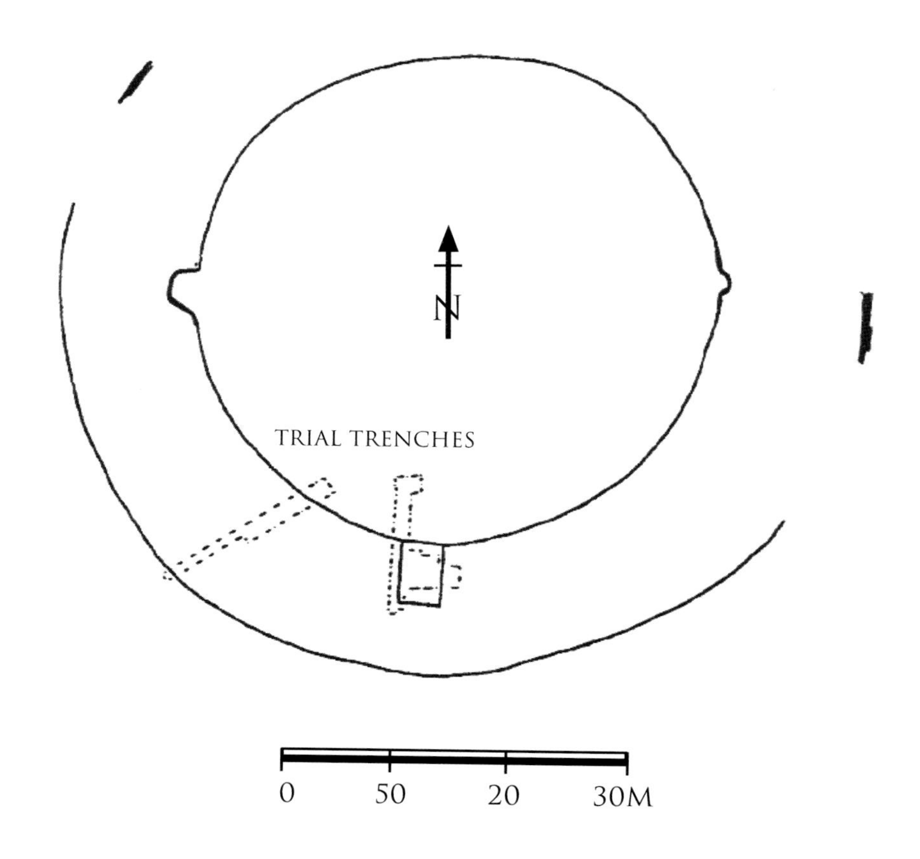

PLAN OF FRILFORD AMPHITHEATRE

2. Hingley, R., Oxford Journal of Archaeology 4 (1985), 205-206
3. Hingley, Britannia 13 (1982), 307
4. Council British Archaeology Grp 9 NL 12 (1982), 150-3
5. Hingley, Oxford Journal of Archaeology 4 (1985), 206
6. Burnham and Wacher, Small Towns of Roman Britain, 182
7. Britannia 13, 305-9
8. Council for British Archeaology Grp 9 NL 12(1982), 150-3

LONDON

London (*Londinium*)
Guildhall Yard
City of London

Map Ref. TQ 3246 8136

How to get here

Follow the street signs in the City of London for 'Guildhall Art Gallery'.
London Underground: Bank, St Paul's, Mansion House and Moorgate.
Car: Limited metered parking is available in the area. There are public car parks on London Wall, Aldersgate and Barbican. There are parking bays for National Orange and Blue Badge holders in Basinghall Street, Gresham Street and Aldermanbury.

Guildhall Art Gallery

Tel: (020) 7332 3700
Fax: (020) 7332 3342
email: guildhall. artgallery@corpoflondon.gov.uk
Website: www.guildhall-art-gallery.org.uk

The Guildhall Art Gallery was established in 1886, in an old building on the east side of Guildhall Yard which had previously been used as Courts of Law. The buildings were badly damaged in bombing during 1940. When they were finally demolished in 1987 Museum of London archaeologists were called to conduct investigations before construction work started. Following discovery of the amphitheatre the new building had to be redesigned, and building construction work only restarted in 1993, continuing, on and off, until shortly before the new Guildhall Art Gallery was opened by the Queen in November 1999.

Entry to the amphitheatre is via Guildhall Art Gallery. Visitors can step into the arena for the first time in nearly 2,000 years. Atmospheric light and sound effects complete the evocative experience. Finds from the site and other excavations in Roman London are displayed at the Museum of London, a short walk away (Museum of London Box Office: (020) 7814 5777).

What you can see

Walking down the entrance way you are flanked by the remains of the stone walls which once stood more than 2m high, and which supported the timber framework for the seating tiers above you. The amphitheatre may have seated more than 5,000 spectators. The walls survive to varying heights because of the often arbitrary way in which the masonry was later 'robbed' for reuse elsewhere.
To get to the sandy arena gladiators and animals used the cobble entranceway passage you are now in. Where the entrance joins the curving arena wall there was once a timber gateway, the threshold beam of which was discovered in the excavation. Doorways gave access from both the arena and the entrance passage into small antechambers. You can see the slots in the stone threshold that imply that one chamber may have had a timber trapdoor, which could be raised to release wild animals.

Hidden beneath the arena floor and under the passageway was a series of wooden drains, complete with a timber-lined settling-tank. The remains are preserved exactly where they have been for about 1,900 years but in a remarkable feat of engineering there are now in fact two basements with offices below you. **1**

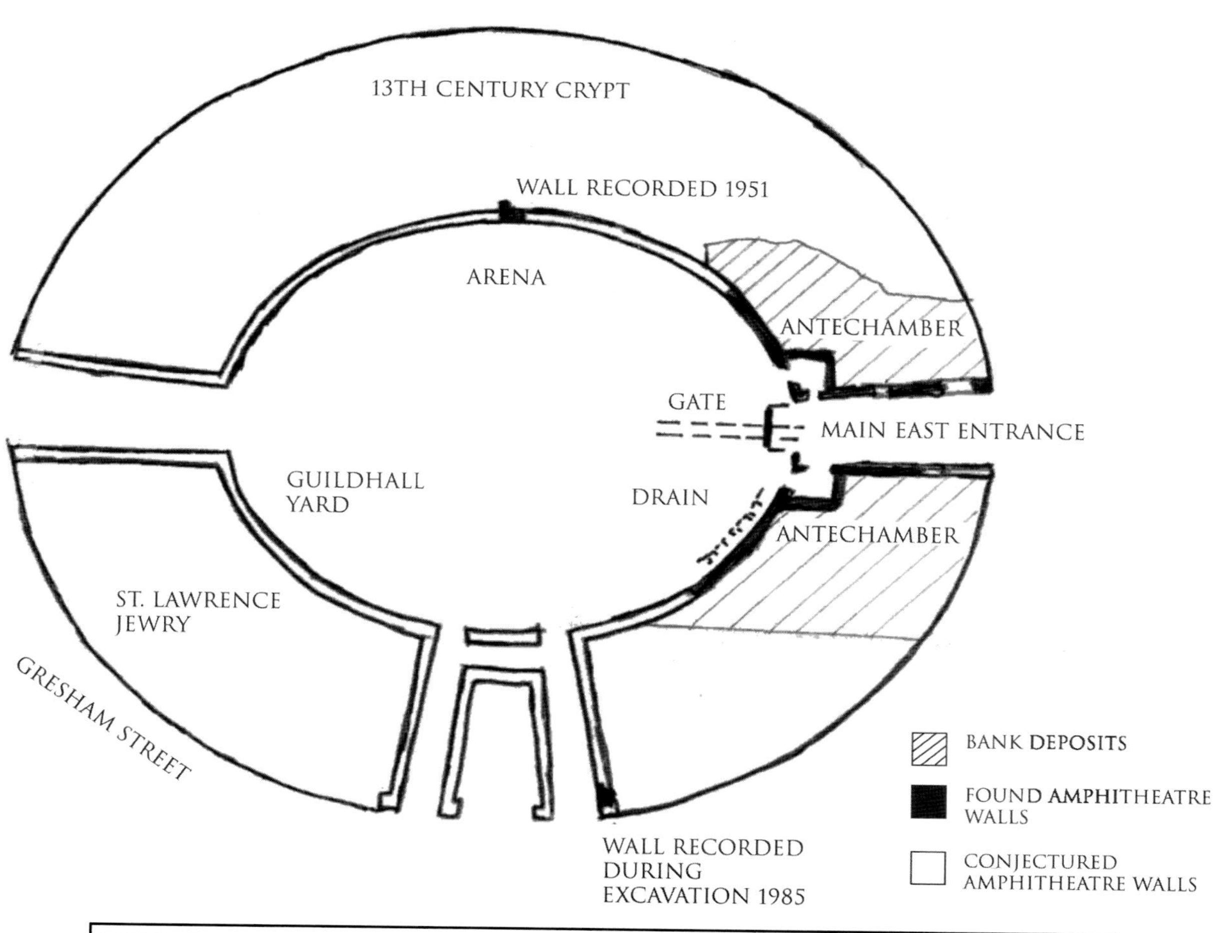

GUILDHALL YARD - INDICATING LINE OF AMPHITHEATRE PHOTO BY MIKE PENNEY
© REPRODUCED BY KIND PERMISSION OF "GUILDHALL ART GALLERY, CORPORATION OF LONDON"

INNOVATIVE PRESENTATION OF THE REMAINS OF THE AMPHITHEATRE IN A "CONTROLLED" ENVIRONMENT
PHOTO BY MIKE PENNEY
© REPRODUCED BY KIND PERMISSION OF "GUILDHALL ART GALLERY, CORPORATION OF LONDON"

Site History & Design Features

After the destruction of *Londinium* by Queen Boudicca in AD 60, it quickly grew to become the most vibrant town in the whole province of Britannia. By the early 2nd century AD, the Roman historian Tacitus was able to describe *Londinium* as 'famous for its wealth of traders and commercial traffic'. It was also at this time that all the major public buildings were put in place: the forum and basilica, the main legal, commercial and financial centre, the public bath and the amphitheatre. **2**

The amphitheatre was first discovered in 1988 when short stretches of Roman wall were observed at the bottom of four archaeological investigation trenches. (Since the dig finished the remains have been protected in a controlled environment in which they could be allowed to dry out slowly, thus preventing damage to the ancient masonry). Unusually, the monument was found to lie within the Roman town. At its construction in AD 70 the amphitheatre lay on the outskirts of the town. However, the Roman fort of Cripplegate was built in about AD 100 at a distance of 30m to the northwest of the amphitheatre. When the city fortifications were reconstructed at the end of the 2nd century AD, dense habitation required that the north-west sector, in which the amphitheatre lay, had to be enclosed with defences. **3**

London's first amphitheatre was first built entirely of wood in AD 70. It underwent a major facelift in the early 2nd century. This involved rebuilding the arena wall and entranceways in tile and ragstone. Elements of brightly-coloured plaster from the arena wall and marble inlays and mouldings from the structure indicate an impressive building. The builders of the amphitheatre took advantage of a natural depression, originally a shallow stream valley. They hollowed the arena out of the valley bottom, disposing the spoil around it to construct seating embankments. **4** The structure lies on an almost east-west alignment **5** and its overall size was 102m by 84m with an arena of 62m by 44m.

The following is a summary of the archaeological excavations carried out:

The scheduled monument is an elliptical ampitheatre, circa 105m long and 85m wide, externally sealed beneath Guildhall Yard and its surrounding buildings. Although located beneath these later buildings, its extent and general ground plan can be discerned from its effect on the topography of this area of the city, in particular where streets established in the tenth and eleventh centuries avoided it. Partial excavations by the Museum of London in 1951, 1985 and 1987-8 have provided much detail on the structural form of the monument. Of particular note is the preservation of timber remains as this was a major material used in the original construction. Features revealed during excavations include an outer wall retaining the seating banks, the inner arena wall and the arena itself, an east entrance with two chambers likely to have been shrines or changing rooms, a porch, plank-lined drains and sumps, timber thresholds and a piled structure round the inside of the arena wall. This work has indicated that the site was in use between the early second century and circa AD 360. By the later fourth century, however, stone was being robbed from the site suggesting it had fallen out of use. After a period of neglect, building began on the site in the early medieval period and has continued down to the present day.

ROMAN WOODEN DRAINS, COMPLETE WITH A TIMBER-LINED SETTLING TANK-EXACTLY AS THEY WHERE C1900. (THERE ARE NOW IN FACT FURTHER BASEMENTS WITH OFFICES BELOW)
PHOTO BY MIKE PENNEY
© REPRODUCED BY KIND PERMISSION OF "GUILDHALL ART GALLERY, CORPORATION OF LONDON"

Notes

129 Guildhall, 1951

A trial-hole revealed a Roman foundation on the E. side of buttress No.3 on the S. side of Guildhall. The mediaeval buttress terminated at a depth of about 3.2m beneath the basement floor of the Comptroller's office, and under it were the remains of a substantial Roman wall, consisting of a course of squared ragstone blocks resting on two courses of bonding-tiles, one of which appeared to be a re-used roofing-tile. Below these was a base of ragstone rubble bound with mortar.

On the S. side of the hole at the same depth was seen a level of broken Roman tiles on a similar base, springing from the N-S. wall, and apparently forming part of an E.-W. wall at right angles to it.

(Sited from map). **6**

Notes

1. The Guildhall Art Gallery Information Booklet, Roman London's amphitheatre
2. *ibid.*
3. Frere, Britannia, 240, 249
4. Bateman, Current Archaeology 137 (1994), 166
5. *Ibid.,* 166
6. Merrifield, R. Roman City of London (1965), 227;
   English Heritage Schedule Entry 23/07/1990

RICHBOROUGH

Richborough (*Rutupiae*)
Dover
Kent

Map ref: TR 3205 5980

How to get here

The site is 2.4km north of Sandwich on a side road off the A257.

Tourist Information

TIC T: 01304 205108

What you can see

Earthwork remains of the Roman amphitheatre associated with the Saxon Shore fort at Richborough survive as an elliptical hollow, about 60m by 50m, measuring 3m deep. The hollow is surrounded by a bank 12m wide and up to 2m high. **1**

Site History & Design Features

As early as 1849 the amphitheatre was partially excavated by Roach Smith. **2** More recently, the earthwork/cropmark remains of the eroded/plough-levelled Roman amphitheatre were mapped at 1: 2500 scale from aerial photographs as part of a multi-disciplinary project (Richborough Environs Project) initiated by English Heritage Aerial photographs:

> The site is located circa 340m to the south west of the Roman fort and appears as an oval enclosure, measuring approximately 80m x 95m, defined by a broad embankment broken by the two entrances to the north-east and south-west. Both entrances are defined by a pronounced thickening and outward bulging of the enclosing embankment. On either side of the embankment, mid-way between the two entrances there appears to be a sub-circular pit or depression cut into the bank of the amphitheatre. It is not clear what these two features represent but they were also noted during the geophysical survey carried out for the project in 2001 by English Heritage Centre for Archaeology. The traces of a World War II gun pit excavated into the SE bank of the amphitheatre were also noted. The mound has been badly eroded by ploughing, but was in very much its present condition when recorded on photographs taken in 1942 and has been under pasture for much of the twentieth century hopefully ensuring no further erosion of the site will occur. **3**

It was once thought that the structure had been built in the third century AD and belonging to a contemporary Saxon Shore fort partly founded on the port's town. **4** However, the building is now considered to have been constructed in about AD 85 when the remaining early Roman military installations were demolished and the nearby civilian settlement underwent improvements. **5**
The amphitheatre was constructed as the developing town's streets were being resurfaced and new shops, workshops, outlying temples and a triumphal monument (the *quadrifrons*) marking the completed conquest of the province by the governor Gnaeus Julius Agricola in 84 AD were built. **6**

The amphitheatre may have belonged to the Type Ib structure category as it exhibits signs of having had entrances leading into the arena on the short axis. The dimensions of the structure were 80m by 66.4m overall with an arena of 60m by 49.8m. **7** The arena wall was 1.05m thick and was largely built of flint, mixed with chalk. The height of the arena wall has not been established but it is certain that its exposed face had been plastered. The plaster was a thick coat of coarse mortar. The banks of the amphitheatre were about 10m wide.

Finds

On the ruined wall of the western entrance a skeleton was found:

> lying on its left side, the legs drawn up and the wrists crossing each other. The place had evidently been hollowed out for its reception: most of the bones of the hands and feet were wanting; but, where the right hand had been, a brass coin of Constans was found. This was a post-Roman burial, possibly of an executed criminal. **8**

Notes

1. NMR Monument Wardens Report TR 35 NW1
2. Smith, C.R., Antiquities of Richborough (1850), 52-3, 161-72
3. Cambridge University collection of aerial photographs catalogue, parts 1-6; parts 7-12; 13-17 & accessions list, 1 by J K St Joseph CUCAP (AFL 13, 18) 14-JUN-1962
   Richborough environs project, Kent: report on the aerial photographic transcription and analysis (2002)
4. Cunliffe, B.W., 'Fifth Report on the Excavations of the Roman Fort at Richborough. Kent' London: Report of the Research Committee of the Society of Antiquaries of London (1968), 248
5. Cunliffe, 'Rutupia', PECS, 778
6. ibid.
7. Cunliffe, Fifth Report on the Excavations of the Roman Fort at Richborough, 248
8. Page W., 'The Victoria history of the county of Kent' 3, The Victoria history of the counties of England, 24-41;
   Dowker, G. 'Archaeologia Cantiana: being contributions to the history and archaeology of Kent', Kent Archaeological Society (1889) 18, 6-14;
   St Joseph, J.K., The Journal of Roman studies (Society for Promotion of Roman Studies), 55 (1965), 88

SILCHESTER

Silchester (*Calleva Atrebatum*) Hampshire

Map ref: SU 6447 6260

How to get here

The site of the Roman town of *Calleva Atrebatum* with its amphitheatre is in open country. It is 16km south of Reading and 10km north of Basingstoke, via side roads 3km northeast of the A340. Park by the church. There is a small site museum west of the town area, near the Rectory at the end of The Drove.

Museums and Tourist information

Silchester Site Museum T: None

Reading Museum Service
The Town Hall
Blagrave Street
Reading
RG1 1QH

T: 0118 939 9800
E: readingmuseum.org.uk

www.mail@readingmuseum.org.uk/silchester

TIC T: 0118 956 6226

What you can see

The amphitheatre is situated about 170m north of the east gate of the third century town. It survives as an earthwork 90m by 75m, comprising two crescent-shaped earthworks surviving to a height of 5.75m, enclosing an oval arena of 46m by 37m. **1** The long axis of the amphitheatre runs 17-20 degrees east of north. **2**

Site History & Design Features

William Stukeley, poet and freemason, first identified the amphitheatre in 1724, but it does not appear to have been excavated before 1979. Excavations between 1979 and 1985 confirmed that the amphitheatre was first constructed during the third quarter of the first century AD, probably between 55 and 75 AD. This amphitheatre underwent three phases of building work.

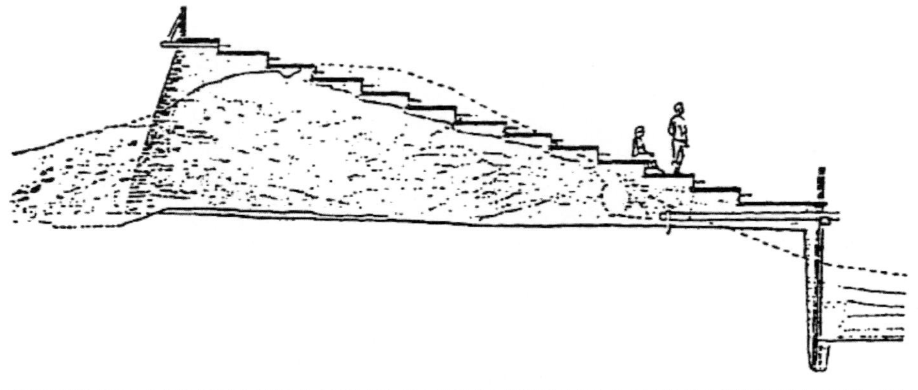

RECONSTRUCTION OF THE TERRACING ON THE SEATING BANK IN THE TIMBER PHASE

During phase I, it was built of timber and consisted of a circular arena with opposing entrances on the north and the south, making it a Type Ia amphitheatre. Spoil from the excavated arena was used to create the seating banks. The seating banks comprised wide shallow steps that probably held simple wooden seating or terraces. The seating capacity has been estimated at between 3,600 and 3,700, or if the spectators stood on the wide terraces, up to 7,250.

A second timber phase of building dates to the mid-second century and included modifications to the arena, changing it to an oval plan.

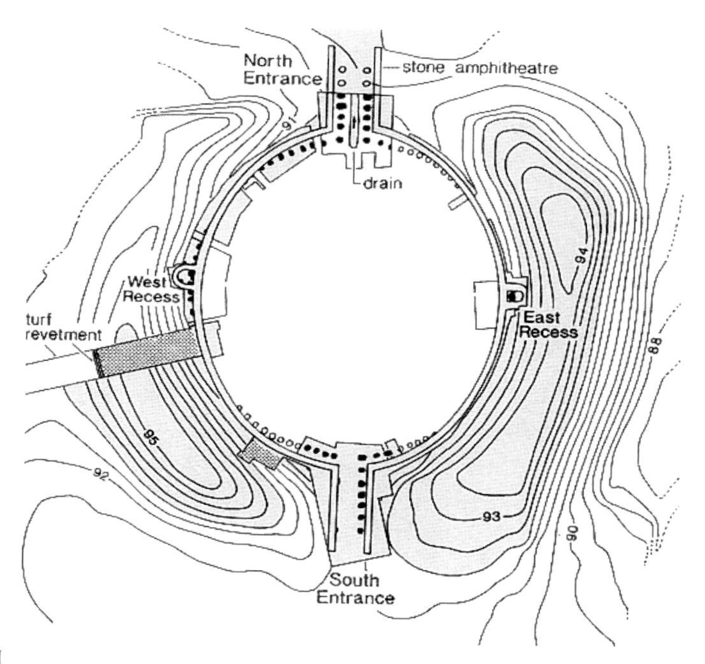

SILCHESTER I

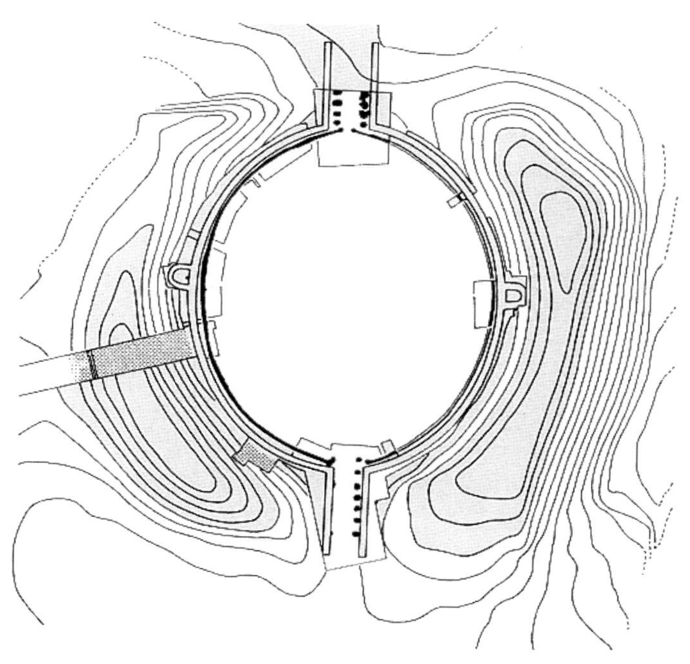

SILCHESTER II

SCALE 1:1000.

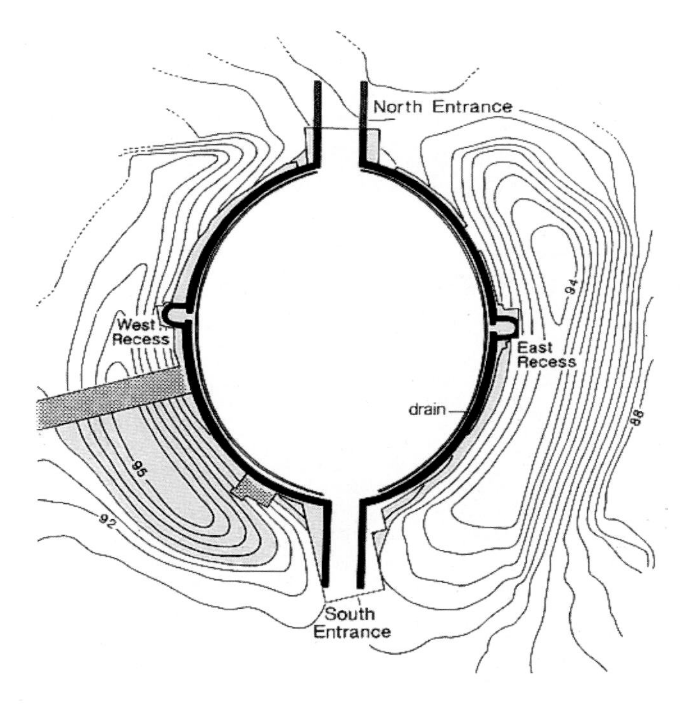

SILCHESTER III SCALE 1:1000.

SILCHESTER I, II & III DIAGRAMS REPRODUCED BY KIND PERMISSION OF PROFESSOR M.G. FULFORD AND THE SOCIETY FOR THE PROMORTION OF ROMAN STUDIES

In phase III, timber was replaced with stone during the early to mid third century AD. The oval shaped arena was retained but enlarged, and the walls of the passages and arena were constructed of flint, probably to a height of 3.75m. The stone walls would have provided support for the lower seating tiers.

Chambers

The amphitheatre was furnished with two roughly rectangular recesses placed directly behind the arena wall at either end of the short axis of the arena. They were accessible only from the arena. It is conjectured that they served another purpose other than as beast pens; the implication is that they may have served as shrines or performer waiting rooms and temporary storage rooms

Post Roman History

There is no evidence of reuse of the amphitheatre area until the late eleventh century to early twelfth century when a single-aisled hall was constructed in the arena; which may have been the Manor House of Silchester at this time. During this period the amphitheatre may have been used as a ringwork, containing the hall and possibly one ancillary building. Traces of one or more possible fighting platforms have also been identified.

From the early fifteenth century until the 1970s the arena had been used as a farmyard for the Mount farmhouse, and had been metalled by the seventeenth century or early eighteenth century. **3**

Roman finds

No finds directly relating to gladiatorial contests were discovered, however for a full discussion of finds see Fulford's report. **4**

Notes

1. NMR Monument Wardens Report SU 66 SW 41
2. Fulford, 'The Silchester Amphitheatre: excavation of 1979-85' in Britannia monograph series 10 (1989). 179
3. M. Fulford, 'The Silchester amphitheatre' – full report.
4. *Ibid.*, 77-159.

AERIAL VIEW OF SILCHESTER AMPHITHEATRE © CROWN COPYRIGHT. NMR

TOMEN-Y-MUR

Tomen-Y-Mur
Maentwrog
North-West Wales

Map ref: SH 7081 3891

How to get here

The amphitheatre is 4km north of Trawsfynydd village and can be reached by a narrow unsigned road to the east of the A470; just a few metres south of the A470/A487 junction (take care; the unsigned turning is very easy to miss!). Go past the Snowdonia National Park sign, cross the cattle grid and the amphitheatre is on the right hand side of the road. The site is 275m above sea level on exposed moorland; be prepared in winter!

Museum

Segontium Roman Museum
Beddgelert Road
Caernarfon
T: 01286 675625

What you can see

An oval embankment enclosure about 39m x 37m externally and 33m x 27m internally now very marshy and with a much depleted earthwork with a boundary wall cutting the western bank.**1** The surviving embankment is about 3m high.

Site History & Design Features

The original name of the fort is not known and it is now generally called Tomen-Y-Mur with reference to the most conspicuous feature of the site, the Norman motte. The name Mur-y-castell in the Mabinogi of Math vab Mathonwy is regarded as referring to this spot. **2**

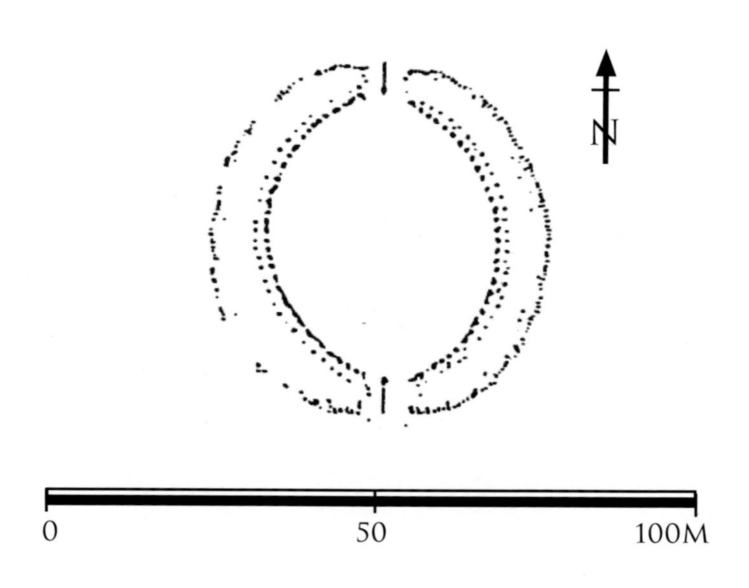

Tomen-Y-Mur is thought to be the only surviving example of an auxiliary amphitheatre in Britain. **3** The auxiliary fort of Tomen-Y-Mur was placed on the slope of a breathtakingly beautiful mountain pass; where it probably served as a station on the main Roman route from North to South Wales which passed nearby. **4**

AERIAL VIEW OF TOMEN-Y-MUR AMPHITHEATRE LOCATED IN LOWER RIGHT HAND SIDE OF PHOTOGRAPH NEAR JUNCTION OF THE ROAD AND FOOTPATH WALLING © SEE FOOTNOTES

The post experienced two phases of Roman occupation, the first probably beginning in the late first century when the region's network of Roman forts and roads was being set up. At about this time, AD 75-85, the fort covered 1.7 hectares; making it the large enough to hold a mixed detachment of cavalry and an infantry *(cohors miliara peditata)*. The fort consisted of earth ramparts topped by a timber palisade. In the second phase of occupation, about AD120-140, its area was reduced to 1.34 hectares, covering the southeast end of the original fort, and it was enclosed with new stone defences. Its evacuation in about AD 140 coincided with that of other Roman auxiliary forts in Wales. **5**

It is likely that the amphitheatre's construction coincided with that of the fort. It lay beyond the parade ground, which was sited northeast of the fort **6** and had a major-axis north-south orientation. **7**

PHOTO BY MIKE PENNEY

PHOTO BY MIKE PENNEY

INSCRIBED ROMAN STONES © SEE FOOTNOTES

Although the amphitheatre has not been excavated, it is certain that the earth embankment comprised the *cavea*, making the monument a Type Ia structure. The material used for the construction of the arena wall is open to conjecture. It may have been timber, or just as likely, local dry-stone walling. It is a curious fact that there are large rectangular dressed slates now dispersed in great number around the area, placed on end as fencing material, in lieu of dry-stone walling. Perhaps these slates may have been used to face the arena wall to provide a smooth finish and were later 'scavenged' by the local farmers for their own use.

Without an excavation of the site, the precise features of the amphitheatre are unknown, except that the arena wall would have retained the front seating bank **8** and that the two *porta pompae* appear to have been the only entrances to the amphitheatre. **9**

Notes

1. Cadw, Monument Wardens report, ME002.
2. Lloyd, J.E., History of Wales, 2398, and Gruffydd, W.J., *Math vab Mathonwey,* 345-7.
3. Collingwood, R.G., The Archaeology of Roman Britain (Methuen and Co. Ltd., 1930), 106; Ralegh Radford, Proceedings of the Llanudno and District Field Club, 17 (1931-3), quoted in C.A. Gresham, 'The Roman Fort at Tomen-Y-Mur', Archaeolgia Cambrensis 93 (1938): 198.
4. Gresham, Archaeologia Cambrensis, 93.
5. Nash-Williams, The Roman Frontier in Wales, 2nd ed., 112-113; Golvin, L'Amphitheatre romain,. 86; Gresham, *Archaeologia Cambrensis* 93 (1938), 208
6. Nash-Williams, The Roman Frontier in Wales, 2nd edition, 113.
7. Gresham, Archaeologia Cambrensis 93 (1938), 198.
8. Golvin, L'Amphitheatre romain, 90.
9. Gresham, Archaeoligia Cambrensis 93 (1938), 198-199.

PHOTO BY MIKE PENNEY

WALTON

Walton
Radnorshire
Wales

Map ref: SO 2522 5994

How to get here

In the community of Old Radnor on private farmland.

What you can see

A circular cropmark feature, about 80-90m in diameter, cut by/cutting a Roman military enclosure. It has been suggested that the feature may have been a Roman gyrus **1** or a horse training area, associated with military settlements to the north. The feature has a possible south-east facing entrance. **2**

Site History

The history and period of the site is unknown at the present time

Notes

1. Gibson, The Walton Basin Project, CBA Research Report 118 (1999).
2. Cadw Monument Wardens report unnumbered

WINTERSLOW

Winterslow
Wiltshire

Map ref: SU 225 329

How to get here

The site is about 1km northeast of Winterslow, just south of the Old Sarum (Salisbury) to Winchester Roman road.

Museum and Tourist information

Salisbury & South Wiltshire Museum
The King's House
65 The Close
Salisbury
SP1 2EN

T: 01722 332151
F: 01722 325611
E: museum@salisburymuseum.org.uk
www.salisburymuseum.org.uk

TIC T: 0172 334956

Remains

Part of a circular earthwork. **1**

Site History

The earthwork was originally identified as a Neolithic long barrow but excavations in 1959, by Mrs. F de Mallet Vatcher, discovered that it was originally circular in plan. It was interpreted as a possible amphitheatre. Neolithic pottery was also recorded.

The excavations indicated that the site was the downhill half of a circular Roman earthwork; the complete circle would have been just under 110m in diameter, taken from outside of the bank. The uphill half was barely visible and had probably been largely destroyed by ploughing.

The part of the circle excavated had been constructed in three superimposed stages. First a levelling platform to counteract the slope of the hill, secondly an irregular core of material scraped up from the surface within the circle, and finally the massive bank itself which was built of grey 'clay', the origin of which is still not wholly determined. This remains to a height of nearly 2.46m from the old surface.

A well had been sunk through the chalk during the building of the final bank. This was excavated to a depth of 18.5m without either water or the bottom being reached. The well was timber-lined and there were the remains of constructional beams round the well head.

There had been a considerable Neolithic occupation of the site; under the earthwork an ancient soil horizon overlay the surface of the chalk, which contained many Windmill Hill and Peterborough sherds. Romano-British pottery was found in and around the bank, and in the well filling. The pottery would appear to be generally late third to fourth century. **2**

Design and Construction

Lack of evidence precludes stating a specific date for the construction of this monument. The earthwork's major axis measured about 110m overall **3** and its orientation was northeast –southwest. The structure was a Type Ia amphitheatre and was built on the side of a dry valley near the foot of the northwestern slope of the steep down on which the modern village of Winterslow is located.

The seating bank of the amphitheatre would have been unusually wide at about 36m. Although the capacity of the amphitheatre has not been calculated, it is clear that it would have been able to accommodate several thousands spectators.

Finds

Contact Salisbury Museum for further information.

Notes

1. NMR Monument Wardens Report SU 23 SW 5
2. The Antiquaries Journal: journal of the Society of Antiquaries of London 43 (1963), 197-213;
   Palmer, R, 'Danebury; an Iron Age hillfort in Hampshire; an arial photographic interpretation of its environs', in Royal Commission on Historical Monuments, England; supplementary series 6, 15
3. Vatcher, Antj 43 (1963), 199.

WOODCUTTS

Woodcutts
Dorset

Map ref: ST 963 181

How to get here

Follow the B3081 westwards from Sixpenny Handley for about 2.4km; immediately past the left turning signposted to Dean and Cashmoor, take the lane to the right. 800m on this lane reaches the earthworks on Woodcutts Common.

Museum and Tourist information

Pitt-Rivers Museum
South Park Road
Oxford
OX1 3PP

T: 01865 270927
F: 01865 270943
E: prm@prm.ox.ac.uk
www.prm.ox.ac.uk

Dorset County Museum
High Street West
Dorchester
DT1 1XA

T: 01305 262735
www.dorsetcountymuseum.org.

Dorset TIC T: 01395 267992

What you can see

Romano-British settlement and earthworks complex excavated and partially reconstructed in the 19th century.**1** Sadly, encroachment by a golf course has resulted in some damage to this attractive site. **2**

Site History

General Pitt-Rivers excavated the site in 1884-5, when it was discovered that although occupation had been continuous, there had been three general phases of occupation dating to the 1st, late 2nd and early 4th centuries. Remains of a bronze casket and a coin hoard consisting of 36 coins dating from 74 BC to about AD 180 or 270 was found; along with burials of thirteen adults, a child killed by a sword-cut, and of twenty-two infants found in pits. Human bones scattered across the site were common. In addition, numerous and varied finds were also recovered, including agricultural and domestic tools.

The excavations showed that, in phase I, the site initially consisted of a circular enclosure, over 92m in diameter and defined by a ditch up to 5.5m wide and 1.85m deep. Trackways led into it and there appear to have been wide gaps in the east, west and north of the structure.

Phase II was characterised by the addition on the west of a kite-shaped enclosure, and two smaller enclosures which contained two corn-drying ovens. Also probably belonging to this phase were two mounds and, perhaps, a barrow since a cremation in a Roman pot was found near it.

In phase III, most of the earlier ditches and pits had been filled and the roughly circular enclosure (seen before the excavation began) had been added on the west. This enclosure contained a well 1.23m in diameter and almost 58m deep, and probably also a building, as evidenced by roofing slabs and painted plaster from wattled walls. Some enclosures from phase II had been retained in phase III. **3**

Design and Construction

The amphitheatre was a Type Ia-earthwork structure and is thought to have held about 1,000 spectators. Its orientation was northwest -southeast and it was constructed on level ground.

Its overall dimensions were about 40m by 30m, with an arena of 21m by 15m. The arena was dug below original ground level. Although elliptical, it was somewhat rounded overall. Two openings leading from the exterior of the monument to the space enclosed by its banks are evident on the main axis of the earthwork. The *cavea* would have been very narrow at only about 10m wide.

One view is that, because of the structure's presence on an ancient road, it may have served as something other than a venue for spectacles. However, an entertainment purpose for the earthwork should not be dismissed, as the roadway may no longer have been in use at the time of construction. **4**

Artefacts Found

The finds are held in the Pitt-Rivers collection and the Dorset County Museum

Notes

1. NMR Monument Wardens Report St 91 NE 24.
2. Johnston, D.E., Discovering Roman Britain (2002), 32.
3. An Inventory of historic monuments in the County of Dorset. 5 (1975): east Dorset, Royal Commission on Historical Monuments (England), 68, 118;
   Pitt-Rivers, Excavations in Cranborne Chase near Rushmore, on the borders of Dorset and Wilts I: 'excavations in the Romano-British village on Woodcutts Common, and Romano-British antiquities in Rushmore Park' (1887), 7-239;
   Hawks, C.F.C, The Archaeological journal 104 (1947), Royal Archaeological Institute, 42-8.
4. Vatcher, Antj 43 (1963), 207-208

GLOSSARY

The Games

andabata (pl. *andabatae*): a gladiator who fought wearing a helmet devoid of eye-holes. He could not see his adversary.

bestiarius (pl. *bestiarii*): a wild beast fighter, typically armed with a knife or spear.

eques (pl. *equites*): a gladiator who fought on a horse. *Equites* were usually pitted against each other in the arena.

essedarius: a gladiator who fought in a chariot. This gladiator's name is derived from *essedum,* the term which denotes a Celtic war-chariot

fuscina: the trident wielded by a *retiarius.*

galerus: the sleeve which covered a *retiarius's* shoulder.

iaculum: t he net wielded by a *retiarius.*

lanista (pl. *lanistae*): a gladiatorial trainer.

ludus (pl. *ludi*): a gladiatorial training school.

munera (sing. *munus*): the spectacles staged in an amphitheatre; the term may also denote gladiatorial shows only.

munera publica (sing. *munus publicum*): games staged by municipal officials or priests as a requirement of office.

munus gladiatorium (pl. *munera gladiatoria*): a gladiatorial exhibition.

naumachia (pl. *naumachiae*): a mock naval battle staged in a flooded arena or on a lake.

pompa: ceremonial procession which paraded in an amphitheatre's arena before a show began.

procurator (pl. *procuratores*) *familiarum gladiatorium:* an imperial official in charge of a province's teams of gladiators.

retiarius (pl. *retiarii*): a gladiator equipped with a net *(iaculum)* and a trident *(fuscina).* He wore only a short tunic, wide belt *(balteus)* and a sleeve on his shoulder *(galerus). Retiarii* fought against *secutores, Samnites* or *murmillones.*

Samnis (pl. *Samnites*): a gladiator equipped with a short sword and long shield. *Samnites* wore a visored helmet decorated with a crest, a sleeve on the right arm, a greave on the left leg and a belt. They are shown fighting *retiarii* on the Borghese Mosaic and the Bignor Mosaic.

secutor (pl. *secutores):* a heavily armed gladiator who usually fought against a *retiarius.* He wore armour and helmet and carried a shield.

venatio (pl. *venationes):* a combat between men and animals or between animals; a *venatio* could also comprise the delivering of criminals to beasts. This type of death sentence was termed *damnatio ad bestias.*

Amphitheatres

amphitheatrum: the term which denoted an amphitheatre in Imperial times.

arena: arena.

balteus: *a* balustrade built on top of an amphitheatre's arena wall serving to protect spectators; the wall of a *praecinctio* or horizontal walkway; or, a wide belt worn by *retiarii* and other gladiators.

carcer (pl. *carceres):* an animal holding pen.

cavea: the seating surrounding an amphitheatre's arena.

cuneus (pl. *cunei):* wedge-shaped block of seats.

euripus: the drain encircling an amphitheatre's arena.

gradus (pl. *gradus*): a tier of seats.

maenianum (pl. *maeniana):* a horizontal zone or storey of seating.

Nemeseum: an amphitheatre shrine dedicated to the goddess Nemesis.

opus incertum: a type of masonry used to face a wall's concrete core consisting of small irregular stones.

pegmata (sing. *pegma):* the winches used to lift animal cages or pieces of decor from the rooms found beneath the arena floor of some amphitheatres.

podium (pl. *podia):* a wide platform located immediately behind an amphitheatre's arena wall. It was intended to accommodate seats of honour.

porta pompae (sing. *porta pompae):* main entrances, located at either end of an amphitheatre's long axis, which provided access to the arena.

portae posticae *(sing.porta postica):* secondary entrances located at either end of an amphitheatre's short axis or elsewhere along the perimeter of the arena wall. They provided access to the arena from the exterior of an amphitheatre or could provide access from the arena to an annular service corridor or small chambers located behind the arena wall.

praecinctio (pl. *praecinctiones):* a walkway between two horizontal zones of seating *(maeniana).*

sacellum (pl. *sacella):* an amphitheatre's shrine.

scalaria: small radial staircases which divided an amphitheatre's seating bank into *cunei* or wedge-shaped seating sections. They permitted spectators to descend to their seats from the *vomitoria* or *praecinctiones.*

spectacula: the term which denoted an amphitheatre in late Republican times.

tribunalia (sing. *tribunal):* boxes found on an amphitheatre's *podium* at either end of the short axis. They were reserved for dignitaries.

velarium: awning protecting the spectators seated in an amphitheatre from the elements.

vomitoria: entrances to the seating. They consisted of doorways in the external wall of an amphitheatre which provided access to internal staircase ascending to the *cavea.*

BIBLIOGRAPHY

Allcrolt, A. Hadrian. Earthwork of England. London: Macmillan and Co., Limited, 1908.

Ashby, T., A. E. Hudd and A. T. Martin. "Excavations at Caerwent, Monmouthshire, on the Site of the Romano-British City of Venta Silurum, in the years 1901-1903," Archaeologia 59 (1904): 87-124.

Auget,Roland. Cruelty and Civilization: The Roman Games. London: George Allen and Unwin Ltd, 1979.

Balsdon, J. P. V. D. Life and Leisure in Ancient Rome. London: the Bodley Head, 1969.

Bateman, Nicholas. "The London Amphitheatre," Current Archaeology no.137 (February 1994): 164-171.

Bell, M. J. B. "Tactical Reform in the Republican Army," Historia 14 (1965): 404-422.

Bomgardner, David L, "The story of the Roman amphitheatre" London (2002): Routledge.

Bomgardner, David L. "Amphitheatres on the fringe," Journal of Roman Archaeology 4 (1991): 282-294.

Bomgardner, David L. "A new era for amphitheatre studies," Journal of Roman Archaeology 6 (1993): 375-390.

Bomgardner, David L. Review of The Silchester Amphitheatre. Excavations of 1979-85 by Michael Fulford, American Journal of Archaeology 95 (1991): 363-364.

Boon, George C. Isca the Roman Legionary Fortress at Caerleon. Mon. Cardiff: National Museum of Wales, 1972.

Boon, George C. and Cohn Williams. Plan of Caerleon: Discoveries to December 1966. Cardiff: National Museum of Wales, 1967.

Bradley, Richard. "Maumbury Rings, Dorchester: the Excavations of 1908-1913," Archaeologia *105 (1976):* 1-97.

Brogen, Olwen. Roman Gaul. London: G. Bell and Sons, Ltd, 1953.

Brown, P. D. C. and Alan D. McWhirr. "Cirencester, 1966," Antiquaries Journal 47(1967): 185-197.

Bunson, Matthew, ed. A Dictionary of The Roman Empire. Oxford: Oxford University Press. 1991.

Burnham, Barry C. and John Wacher. The Small Towns of Roman Britain. Berkeley: University of California Press, 1990.

Collingwood, R. G The Archaeology of Roman Britain. London: Methuen and Co. Ltd., 1930.

Collingwood, R. G. And J. N. L. Myres. Roman Britain and the English Settlements. 2nd ed. Oxford: The Clarendon Press, 1968.

Collingwood, R. G. and Ian Richmond. The Archaeology of Roman Britain. 2nd ed. London: Methuen and Co. Ltd, 1969.

Collingwood, R. G. and T. V. Taylor. "Roman Britain in 1930," Journal of Roman Studies 21 (1931): 224.

Collingwood, R. G. and T. V. Taylor. "Roman Britain in 1931," Journal of Roman Studies 22 (1932): 205.

Crook, J. A., Andrew Linlott and Elizabeth Rawson, eds. The Cambridge Ancient History vol. 9. Cambridge: Cambridge University Press, 1994.

Cunliffe, B. W., ed. Fifth Report on the Excavations of the Roman Fort at Richborough. Kent.

London: Report of the Research Committee of the Society of Antiquaries of London, 1968.

Davies, R. W. "Fronto, Hadrian and the Roman Army," Latomus 27 (1968): 75-95.

Davies, R. W. "Roman military training grounds," Roman Frontier Studies 1969. Edited by Eric Birley, Brian Dobson and Michael Jarrett. Cardiff: University of Wales Press, 1974.

Davies, R. W. "Training Grounds of the Roman Cavalry," The Archaeological Journal 125 (1968): 73-100.

Drinkwater, J. F. Roman Gaul: The Three Provinces. 58 BC-AD 260. London: Croom Helm, 1983.

Frere, Sheppard. "Roman Britain in 1987," Britannia 19 (1988): 461-462.

Frere, Sheppard. Britannia. London: Routledge and Kegan Paul, 1967.

Frere, Sheppard. Britannia. 3rd ed. London: Routledge and Kegan Paul, 1987.

Friedlander, Ludwig. Roman Life and Manners under the Early Empire. 4 vols. 7th ed. Translated by J. H. Freese, Leonard A. Magnus and A. B. Gough. London: George Routledge and Sons, Limited, 1928.

Fulford, Michael. "Excavations on the Sites of the Amphitheatre and Forum-Basilica at Silchester, Hampshire: an interim report," Antiquaries Journal 65 (1985): 39-8 1.

Fulford, Michael. The Silchester Amphitheatre: Excavations of 1979-85. London: Britannia Monograph Series no.10, 1989.

Giles, J. A, ed. and trans. Six Old English Chronicles. London: George Bell and Sons, 1891.

Golvin, Jean-Claude. L'amphitheitre romain: essai sur la theorisation de sa forme et de ses functions. 2 vols. Paris: Publications du centre Pierre Paris, 1988.

Gray, H. St. George. "Excavations at the 'Amphitheatre,' Charterhouse-on-Mendip, 1909," Proceedings of the Somersetshire Archaeological and Natural History Society 55 (1910): 118-137.

Gresham, C. A. "The Roman Fort at Tomen-y-mur," Archaeologia Cambrensis 93(1938): 192-211.

Hammond, N. 0. L. and H. H. Scullard, eds. The Oxford Classical Dictionary. 2nd ed. Oxford: The Clarendon Press, 1970.

Harden, D. B., K. S. Painter, R. H. Pinder-Wilson and Hugh Tait. Masterpieces of Glass. London: The British Museum, 1968.

Harden, Donald B. Glass of the Caesars. Milan: Olivetti, 1987.

Hingley, R. "Location, Function and Status: A Romano-British 'Religious Complex' at the Noah's Ark Inn, Frilford (Oxfordshire)," Oxford Journal of Archaeology 4 (1985): 201-214.

Hingley, Richard. "Recent Discoveries of the Roman Period at the Noah's Ark Inn, Frilford, South Oxfordshire," Britannia 13 (1982): 305-309.

Horne, Eileen A. "Air Reconnaissance, 1975-1977," Aerial Archaeology 1(1977): 16-20.

Jennison, 0. Animals for Show and Pleasure in Ancient Rome. Manchester: Manchester University Press, 1937.

King, Anthony. Roman Gaul and Germany. Berkeley: The University of California Press, 1990.

Lepper, Frank and Sheppard Frere, eds. Trajan's Column: A New Edition of the Cichorius Plates. Gloucester: Alan Sutton Publishing, 1988.

Little, J. H. "The Carmarthen Amphitheatre," Carmarthenshire Antiquary 7 (1971): 58-63.

"The London Amphitheatre," (compiled by editors) Current Archaeology no.109 (April 1988): 49-
50.

MacDonald, William L. The Architecture of the Roman Empire 11: an urban appraisal. New Haven: Yale University Press, 1986.

MacKendrick, Paul. The Dacian Stones Speak. Chapel Hill: The University of North Carolina Press, 1975.

Maxwell, G.S. and D. R. Wilson. "Air Reconnaissance in Roman Britain 1977-84," Britannia 18 (1987): 148.

Millett, Martin. The Romanization of Britain. Cambridge: Cambridge University Press, 1992.

Moloney, Colm. "Catterick Race Course," Current Archaeology no.148 (June 1996): 128-132.

Nash-Williams, V. E. The Roman Frontier in Wales. 2nd ed. Edited by Michael 0. Jarrett.
Cardiff: University of Wales Press, 1969.

Painter, K. S. "A Roman Bronze Helmet from Hawkedon, Suffolk," British Museum Ouarterly 33 (1969): 121-130.

Potter, T. W. and Catherine Johns. Roman Britain. Berkeley: The University of California Press, 1992.

Rich, Anthony. A Dictionary of Roman and Greek Antiquities. 4th ed. London: Longmans, Green, and Co., 1874.

Richmond, 1. A. Review of The Legionarv Fortress at Caerleon. Monmouthshire by V. E. Nash-Williams, Journal of Roman Studies 31 (1941): 215.

Richmond, I. A. Roman Britain. London: Jonathan Cape, 1963.

Richmond, 1. A. "Trajan's Army on Trajan's Column," Papers of the British School at Rome 13 (1935): 1-40

"Roman Britain in 1934," (compiled by editor) Journal of Roman Studies 25 (1935): 208.

Scullard, H. H. Roman Britain: Outpost of the Empire. London: Thames and Hudson Ltd, 1979.

Seilman, R. R. Roman Britain. London: Methuen and Co. Ltd., 1956.

Smith, Gary E. A Guide to the Roman Amphitheatres. Los Angeles: Westland Printing Co., Inc., 1984.

Stiliwell, Richard, William L. MacDonald and Marian Holland McAllister, eds. Princeton Encyclopedia of Classical Sites. Princeton, New Jersey: Princeton University Press, 1976.

Taylor, T. V. and R. G. Collingwood. "Roman Britain in 1926," Journal of Roman Studies 16 (1926): 217.

Taylor, T. V. and R. G. Collingwood. "Roman Britain in 1929," Journal of Roman Studies 19 (1929): 192-193.

Thompson, F. H. "The Excavation of the Roman Amphitheatre at Chester," Archaeologia 105 (1976): 127-239.

Thompson, F. H. The Roman Amphitheatre at Chester. Edinburgh: Department of Environment, 1972.

Thompson, F. H. Roman Cheshire. Chester: Cheshire Community Council, 1965.

Todd, M. Roman Britain: 55 BC-AD 400. London: Fontana Paperbacks, 1981 (fourth impression, 1990).

Toynbee, J. M. C. Animals in Roman Life and Art. London: Thames and Hudson, 1973.

Toynbee, J. M. C. Art in Britain Under the Romans. Oxford: The Clarendon Press, 1964.

Toynbee, J. M. C. Art in Roman Britain. London: Phaidon Press Ltd, 1963.

Vatcher, Faith de Mallet. "The Excavation of the Roman Earthwork at Winterslow, Wilts." Antiquaries Journal 43 (1963): 197-213.

Wacher, John. The Towns of Roman Britain. London: B.T. Batsford Ltd., 1974.

Wacher, John. The Towns of Roman Britain. 2nd ed. London: B. T. Batsford Ltd., 1995.

Wacher, John S. "Cirencester 1962: Third Interim Report," Antiquaries Journal 43 (1963): 15-26.

Wacher, John S. "Cirencester 1963: Fourth Interim Report," Antiquaries Journal 44 (1964): 9-18.

Ward, John. The Roman Era in Britain. 3rd ed. London: Methuen and Co. Ltd., 1920.

Ward, John. Romano-British Buildings and Earthworks. London: Methuen and Co. Ltd., 1911.

Ward-Perkins, J. B. Roman Imperial Architecture. Harmondsworth, Middlesex: Penguin Books Ltd, 1981.

Watson, G. R. The Roman Soldier. London: Thames and Hudson, 1969.

Webster, Graham. The Roman Imperial Army. London: Adam and Charles Black, 1979.

Welch, Katherine. "Roman amphitheatres revived," Journal of Roman Archaeology 4 (1991): 271-281.

Welch, Katherine. "The Roman arena in late-Republican Italy: a new interpretation," Journal of Roman Archaeology 7 (1994): 59-80.

Wheeler, R. E. M. and T. V. Wheeler. "The Roman Amphitheatre at Caerleon, Monmouthshire," Archaeologia 28 (1928): 111-218.

White, G.M. "The Chichester Amphitheatre: Preliminary Excavations," Antiquaries Journal 16 (1936): 149-159.

Wiedemann, Thomas. Emperors and Gladiators. London: Routledge, 1992.

Wilkes, J. J. Dalmatia. Cambridge, Massachusetts: Harvard University Press, 1969.

Wilson, D. R. "Roman Britain in 1960," Journal of Roman Studies 51 (1961): 165-167.

Wilson, D. R. "Roman Britain in 1962, 1: Sites Explored," Journal of Roman Studies 53 (1963): 125-159.

Wilson, D. R. "Roman Britain in 1963, 1: Sites Explored," Journal of Roman Studies 54 (1964): 152-177.

Wilson, D. R. "Roman Britain in 1965," Journal of Roman Studies 56 (1966): 200-201.

Wilson, D. R. "Roman Britain in 1966," Journal of Roman Studies 57 (1967): 174-202.

Wilson, D. IL "Roman Britain in 1967," Journal of Roman Studies 58 (1968): 183-184.

Wilson, D. IL "Roman Britain in 1968, I: Sites Explored," Journal of Roman Studies 59(1969): 198-34.

Wilson, D.R. "Roman Britain in 1970, I: Sites Explored", Britannia 2 (1971): 242-288